Massiv

A Solo Female Wanderer Hiking Guide

Massiv, A Solo Female Wanderer Hiking Guide. ISBN 978-1-961878-26-6 for paperback. Copyright 2024 by Sarah Rowe. For more information about this hiking guide and others, email hi@solofemalewanderer.com

A portion of the proceeds from the sale of this guide is donated to DNT to support their work maintaining the trail system and cabins.

Introduction

Massiv is one of Norway's signature long hikes, going 350 kilometers through four national parks. It's a test of mental and physical strength – it's eighteen days across plains, glaciers, alpine bowls, and everything in between.

I did it in summer 2022 and fell in love with Norway's landscapes and incredible public cabin system. The hike goes from cabin to cabin, enabling you to meet other hikers every night and sleep in a dry bed.

Table of Contents

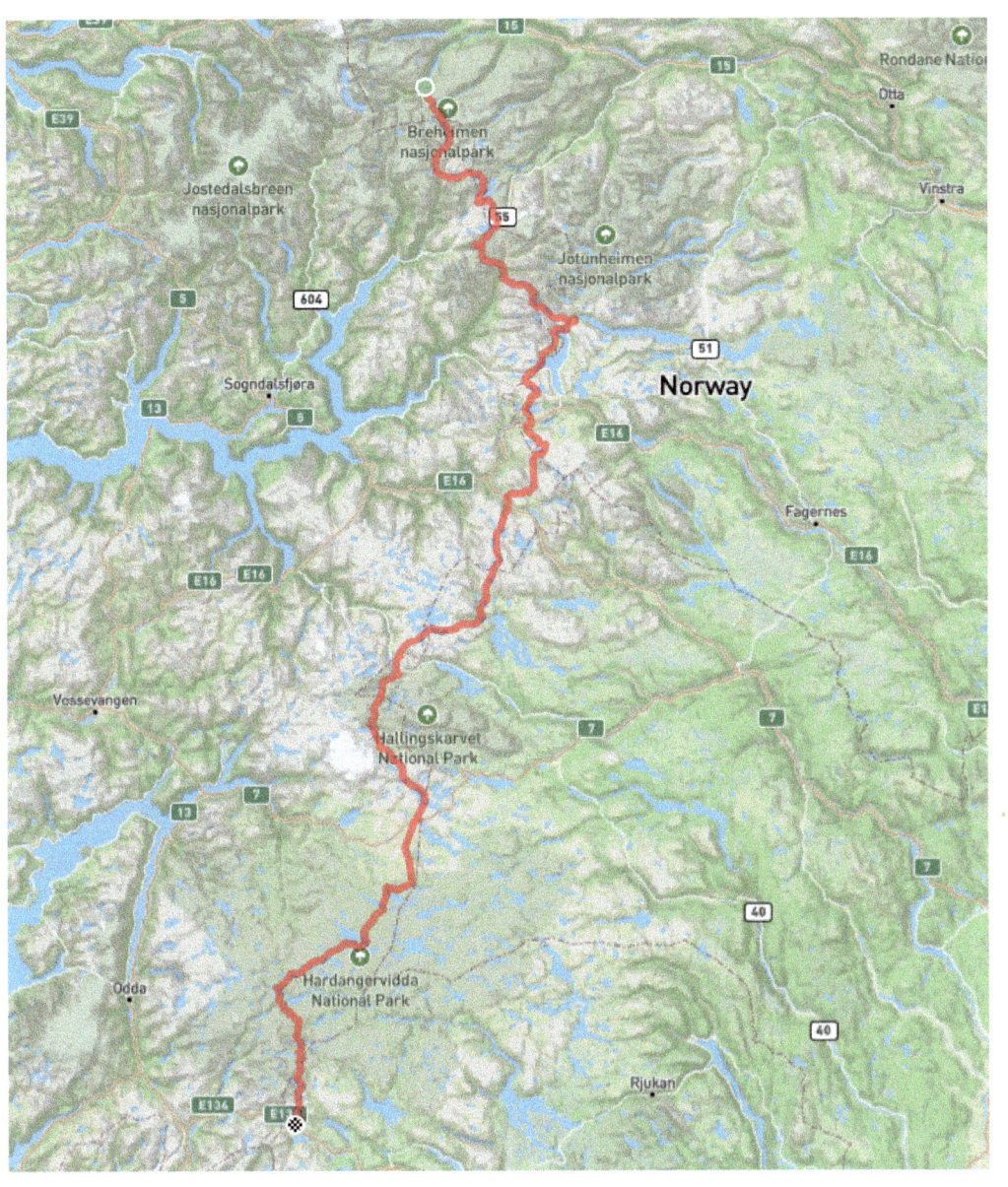

The Day by Day Plan

Hike day	Route	Stage
0	Arrive at Sota Sæter	Breheimen
1	Sota Sæter - Nørdstedalseter	Breheimen
2	Nørdstedalseter - Sognefjellshytta	Breheimen
3	Sognefjellshytta - Fannaråken	Jotunheimen
4	Fannaråken - Skogadalsbøen	Jotunheimen
5	Skogadalsbøen - Fondsbu	Jotunheimen
6	Fondsbu - Slettningsbu	Jotunheimen
7	Slettningsbu - Sulebu	Skarvheim
8	Sulebu - Skarvheim	Skarvheim
9	Skarvheim - Bjordalsbu	Skarvheim
10	Bjordalsbu - Iungsdalshytta	Skarvheim
11	Iungsdalshytta - Kongshelleren - Geiterygghytta	Skarvheim
12	Geiterygghytta - Finse	Skarvheim
13	Finse - Krækkja	Hardangervidda
14	Krækkja - Stigstuv	Hardangervidda
15	Stigstuv - Sandhaug	Hardangervidda
16	Sandhaug - Litlos	Hardangervidda
17	Litlos - Hellevassbu	Hardangervidda
18	Hellevassbu - Haukeliseter	Hardangervidda

Massiv crosses four national parks; it's possible to split up the hike into sections and do one national park at a time. The sections get progressively easier

Length (km)	Elevation Gain (m)	Elevation Drop (m)	Hours (from ut.no)
-	-		-
25.4	1,333	1,065	10 to 12
26.5	959	570	10 to 12
14.4	489	126	5 to 7
11.9	363	1,217	6
24.8	1,129	1,015	8
24.3	684	430	6
16.5	520	505	6
19.0	529	833	6
13.0	613	104	5
16.0	346	826	6
28.9	974	861	10
16.1	421	477	5.5
24.4	797	843	8
20.0	446	366	6
23.0	215	203	6
25.6	283	326	8
16.0	469	488	5.5
21.0	565	763	7

UT.no is run by the Norwegian Trekking Association (DNT) and gives time estimates for an average Norwegian hiker carrying a backpack

Sota Sæter to Nørdstedalseter

| 25.4 km | 1,333 meters | 1,065 meters | 10 hours |
| 15.8 miles | 4,373 feet | 3,493 feet | Very challenging |

The day starts with a climb up to a ridge overlooking Sota Sæter, the longest climb on the route. There's about 850 meters of elevation gain before you hit the top of the ridge. After the climb, you'll start to go along the Illvatnet (-vatnet translates to "the lake") in very rocky terrain. This section is very slow going since you'll be scrambling over rocks - there's also limited or no cell phone service in this section. Eventually, you'll clear the rocky section and start the hike down towards Nørdstedalseter, passing a smaller lake used for hydroelectric power. Eventually, you reach the cabin on a construction road.

My hiking notes:

Especially on the way up, take plenty of breaks. The view behind you is the most impressive view, so turn around and check it out when you need to catch your breath.

The hosts at Nørdstedalseter know that this is a long hike and will serve dinner until late. If you arrive after 10pm or so, you might need to make your own dinner in the self-service cabin attached to Nørdstedalseter, but you won't have to go hungry.

If you're really worried about time, you can consider going over Arentzbu and Sprongdalshytta (see the Massiv extensions on page 46). It will add two days to the trip, but the hikes will each be closer to 6 hours/day instead of 10-12.

Two tactical tips - first, screenshot the weather forecast before you leave Sota Sæter. There is no phone service at Nørdstedalseter, and the next day's hike is equally demanding. Second, don't get confused by some signs saying "Nørstedalseter" and others saying "Nørdstedalseter". UT.no and DNT use both spellings.

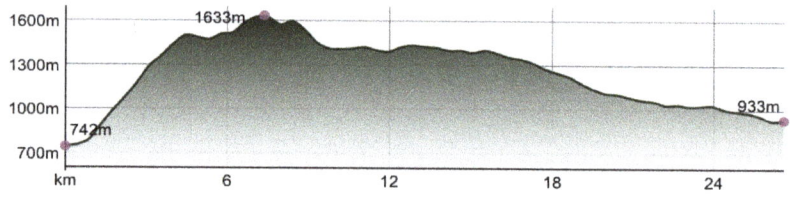

This is one of the two hardest days of Massiv. Don't get discouraged if it feels much slower and more difficult than you initially anticipated – part of the mental challenge of Massiv is getting through the first two days.

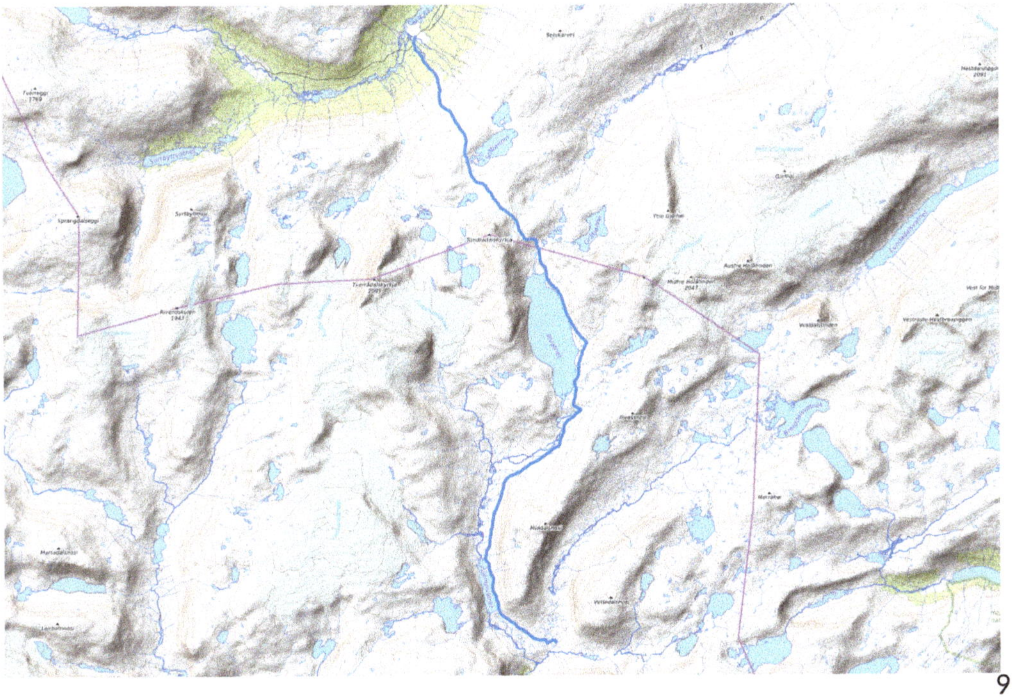

Nørdstedalseter to Sognefjellshytta

26.5 km **16.4 miles**	**959 meters** **3,146 feet**	**570 meters** **1,871 feet**	**10-12 hours** **Very challenging**

This is the hardest day on Massiv. The trail starts out climbing up Vetledalen on a construction road, one of the steepest climbs on Massiv. Pass the trail that turns off towards Stølsdalen and continue along the road, then continue to the northeast on the north side of a lake, Nedre Grønevatnet. Continue climbing all the way up to Tverrbyttfjellet at 1,571 meters above sea level. Depending on snow melt, you may need to wade over a river in this section. After reaching Tverrbyttfjellet and going around the Liabrevatnet, you'll turn towards the southeast. The trail becomes much rockier through this area, and there will often be snowfields into August.

The trail starts to go towards the west of Storevatnet, a large body of water (literally, the name means "the big water"). It is very rocky through this section and will be very difficult if it's rained. Eventually, the trail towards the east and starts to climb along the front of the dam at the southern end of Storevatnet. From here, the trail climbs slightly, then turns towards the south and drops down to Sognefjellshytta on dirt trails.

My hiking notes:

This one is a doozy. I made the mistake of doing it on a day with pouring rain and freezing fog, and it may have been the toughest hike of my life. I built a lot of character, but I wouldn't do it in that kind of weather again. Especially if you're tired, you might want to wait a day at Nørdstedalseter for good weather.

You get up to high elevation during the day, so make sure to have your layers handy. I ended up using a hat and socks on my hands when I did it, even before the weather turned. I also recommend poles for the snowfields.

On the good news side - Sognefjellshytta has a buffet dinner that goes until nine at night, so you'll get fed even if you get there late. And the first two days are the toughest, so it's going to get better from here!

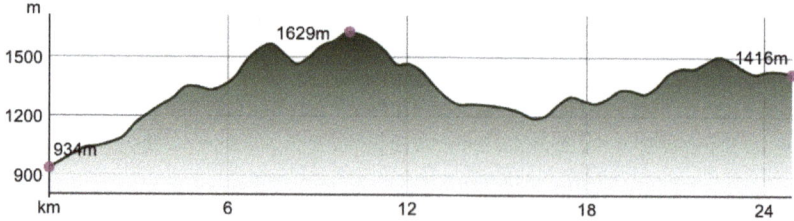

Be prepared for snowfields in the first half of the day - it's often tough to spot the trail under the snow

11

Sognefjellshytta - Fannaråken

14.4 km
9.0 miles

489 meters
1,605 feet

126 meters
415 feet

5-7 hours
Challenging

Today starts with a relatively short hike to the base of the Fannaråk glacier, over a pretty straightforward trail. There's not a ton of elevation gain on the first part, and the trail is much less rocky than the previous days.

You'll meet the guide and the rest of the group going up the glacier at the base of the glacier after about six kilometers of hiking. The trail can be hard to spot for the last kilometer, so follow other people if you can. Once you're at the base of the glacier, wait for the guides to come down and give everyone instructions, then you'll then go over the glacier roped in together. If you're lucky enough to have good weather, the views are spectacular.

Once you finish crossing the glacier, there are two kilometers left of climb to reach the cabin. This section is rockier than the morning, but still less rocky than the previous days.

You need to book Fannaråkhytta in advance, since they have a very limited number of beds. You'll also need to book guiding over the glacier, which you can do either at the reception at Sognefjellshytta or by calling the cabin in advance. The cabin staff all speak English.

My notes

I did this hike after two days of pouring rain, which meant that what would have been the straightforward trail was actually a lot of wading for me. I recommend bringing an extra snack and something warm to drink for the wait at the bottom of the glacier. I waited for close to 45 minutes before the guides arrived and started the equipment demonstration, and having an extra drink kept me from getting grouchy. I'd also put on all your extra layers if it's cloudy - it was much colder on the glacier than I expected. The group goes at the pace of the slowest hiker in the group, so I wasn't hiking fast enough to generate a lot of body heat.

Be mentally prepared for the last two kilometers after the glacier - I wasn't. For some reason, I thought the guided section would drop me right at the cabin, and I wasn't ready for the last bit of the climb.

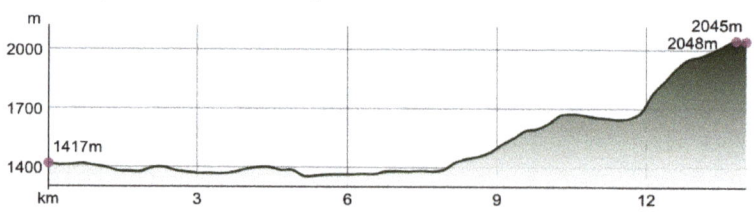

Fannaråkhytta has much more limited facilities than the other DNT serviced cabins - there are no showers, no kiosk for supplies, no place to dispose of trash, and a very basic drying room. Stock up at Sognefjellshytta if you need anything.

I had minimal phone service at the cabin, and there were many spots without service on the hike.

This little spur is from me going the wrong way – make sure to check the map. There are lots of lakes, and I confused two of them

13

Fannaråken - Skogadalsbøen

| 11.9 km | 363 meters | 1,217 meters | 6 hours |
| 7.4 miles | 1,190 feet | 3,993 feet | Challenging |

Today is entirely downhill, a change from the last few days. The first part of the day is slow going as the trail goes through steep, rocky downhills, as well as snowfields. Once you pass through the rocky section and the snowfields, you enter an alpine meadow where you continue to steeply drop . Once you finish dropping down through the meadow, you'll cross a bridge, then go about a kilometer to Skogadalsbøen. This part of the trail is thankfully flat and easy to navigate.

My hiking notes

I thought that this was going to be an easy day because it was all downhill. It was not. This is a very steep descent, starting in a rocky section and then going on a dirt trail. I ended up being slower on the downhill than I was on the uphill on the previous days. In retrospect, I would have left Fannaråkhytta later and taken this more slowly.

Watch out for snow bridges when you're crossing over rivers. I met someone in the cabin who'd fallen through one and was soaking wet.

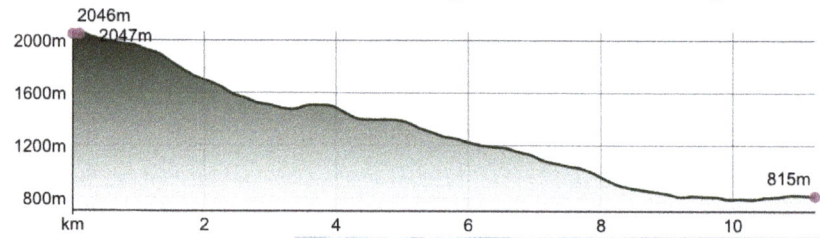

There's no phone service, so check messages and the weather forecast on the way. But Skogadalsbøen does have one of the most effective drying rooms I've used.

Skogadalsbøen - Fondsbu

24.8 km
15.4 miles

1,129 meters
3,703 feet

1,105 meters
3,331 feet

8 hours
Challenging

Today starts with a climb up to Uradalsbandet, a saddle, at 1,400 meters. From here, you should have a great view towards Uranostind at 2,157 meters, assuming that it's not raining. It's a straightforward trail, dirt most of the time. After this, you'll hike along a lake with small rocks, much easier than the previous few days. It's fairly flat through this section until you hit about kilometer twenty and start the drop down to Fondsbu through a meadow. The trail to Fondsbu can be a little difficult to follow, as there are private cabins around Fondsbu. I chose to drop straight down on the marked T path and then take the road to Fondsbu, but you can also take smaller, unmarked trails to Fondsbu.

My hiking notes:

The first part of the hike has a lot of plant life on it, so if it's been raining, wear rain pants or gaiters to keep water from getting into your shoes. Overall, the terrain isn't nearly as bad as the days before it - even the rocky section feels less rocky than before.

Solbjørg Kvålshaugen, who runs Fondsbu, is a celebrity among outdoor lovers in Norway. She sings a song for all of the guests before dinner, and it's one of the highlights of staying in the cabin system. Fondsbu also had the most delicious cabbage I've ever eaten (and cabbage is not usually a food that inspires gushing praise). To be honest, it will feel like a luxury hotel after a few days of being in the wilderness. There are even indoor flush toilets and wifi.

If you need to get back into civilization, there is a bus during the summer from Fondsbu that connects to bus service to Oslo.

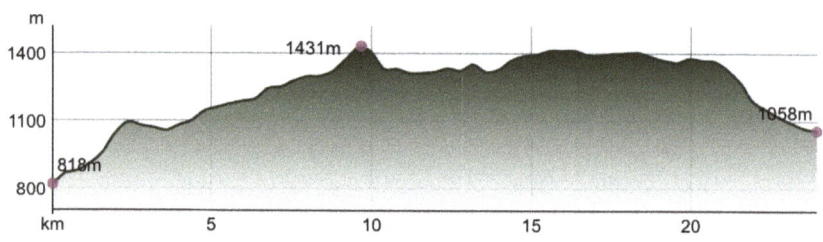

Not in the picture: an unlucky couple whose tent had started to blow away

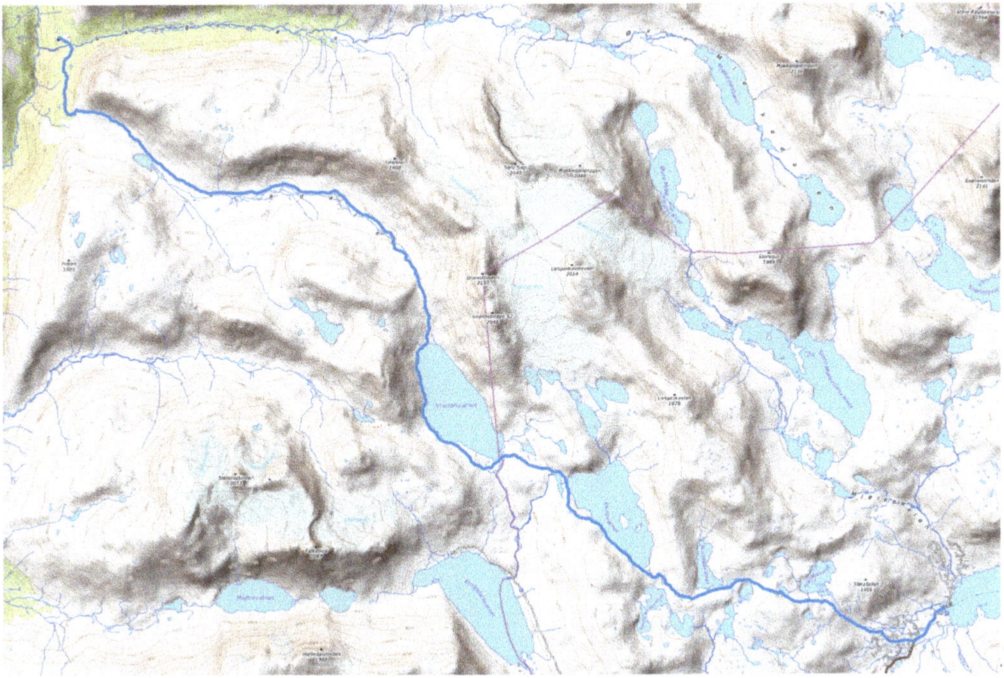

Fondsbu - Slettningsbu

24.3 km
15.1 miles

684 meters
2,244 feet

430 meters
1,410 feet

6 hours
Challenging

From Fondsbu, you start today's hike following the road to Tyinholmen. Pass Tyinholmen after about three kilometers of hiking and continue along the road for a few hundred meters, then turn off to the west as the road starts to gain elevation. You'll continue to follow this trail until you get to a flat section along the edge of Tyin lake. This section is easy in dry weather, but very wet in damp weather - I needed gaiters and to test every step to make sure I wasn't stepping into a puddle. After the lake, you'll reach the Fv53 road, which you'll walk along for a kilometer before turning left (towards the south) and walking up through a small collection of cabins. It's a little bit difficult to find the trail through here, so check UT frequently.

From here, it's three kilometers of climb in gentle terrain until you reach Slettningsbu along the Øvre Årdalsvatnet lake at 1,313 meters above sea level.

My hiking notes

I thought this would be a relatively easy day because of the elevation profile and distance, but I again underestimated the weather. The morning is a little bit boring as you go along the road to Tyin. Once you're on the trail, it's either swampy or lovely, just depending on how much rain there's been recently. I had swampy, and I was very thankful to get to Slettningsbu.

Slettningsbu doesn't have a drying room or showers, but others in the cabin jumped in the lake to wash off. There are also racks above the fireplace for drying out clothes.

18

m
1346m
1300
1100
1059m
km
5
10
15
20

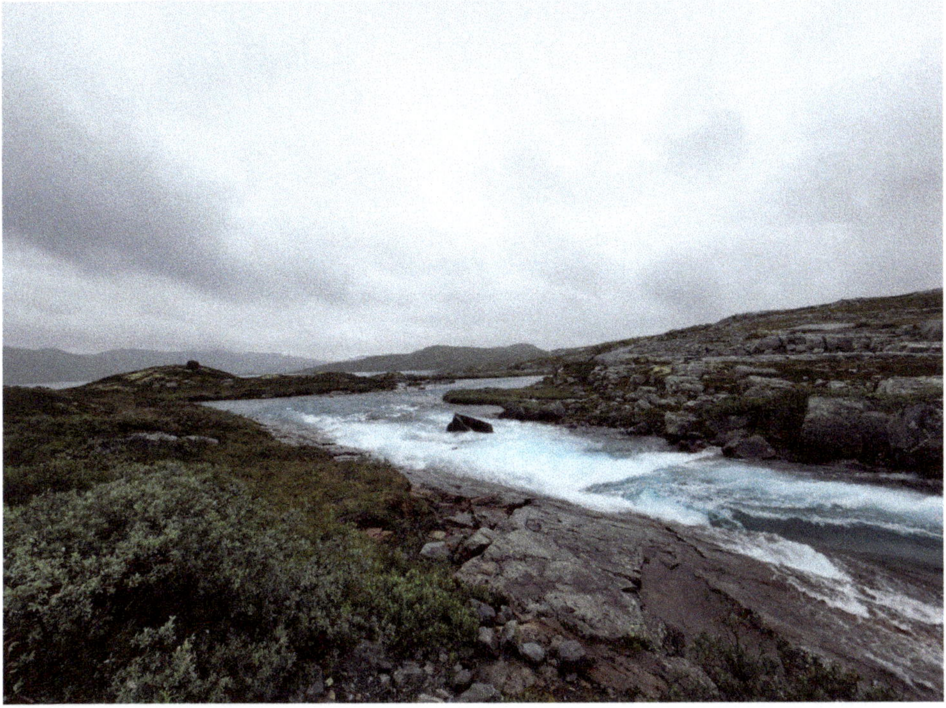

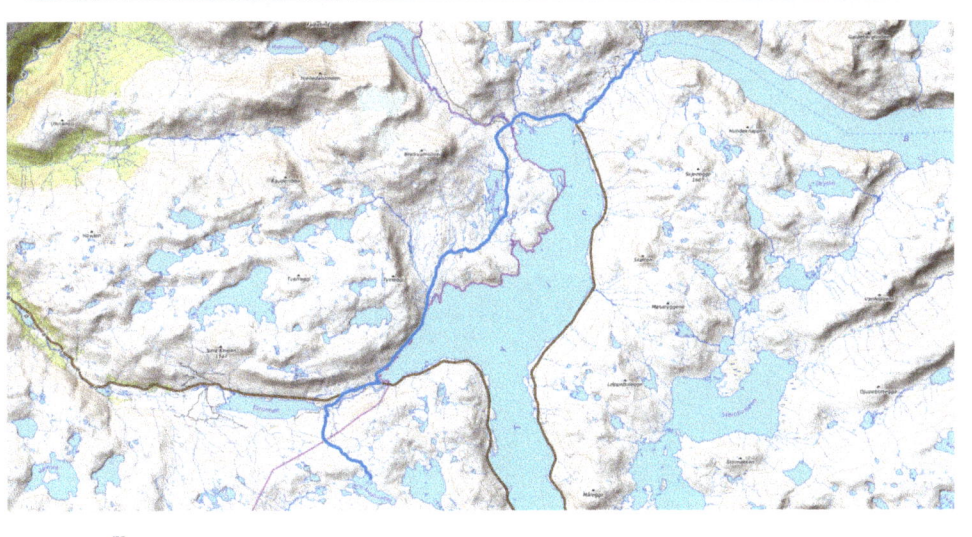

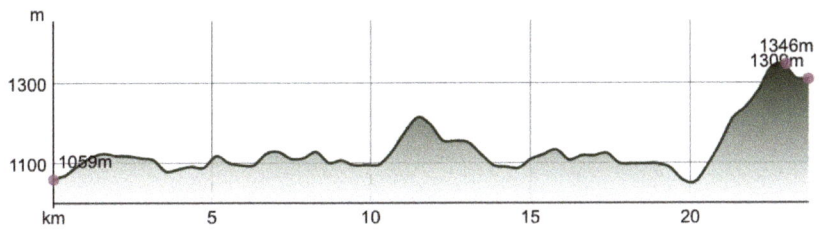

Slettningsbu - Sulebu

16.5 km	520 meters	505 meters	6 hours
10.3 miles	1,706 feet	1,657 feet	Challenging

Start the day following a trail along the lake, until the Øvre Årdalsvatnet lake ends and the trail veers southwest towards Slettningen. Be sure to check that you have the right trail - there are numerous trails branching off from near Slettningsbu. The terrain is easy to cross in this area - dirt trails and not many rocks. After this, you'll drop towards Kyrkjestølen. From here, at about ten kilometers of total hiking, cross the road and start going up the other side, first climbing and then walking across flat terrain. It's eight kilometers from the road to Sulebu, in easy to cross terrain.

My hiking notes

The note about checking where you're going comes from my mistake at the beginning off the trail - I got so excited about sunny weather and a bit of a rest day that I took off in the wrong direction for more than two kilometers.

The terrain is much easier in this section than in Breheimen and Jotunheimen. I ended up doing day 7 and 8 as a double and don't recommend it - it was more than a marathon worth of hiking, and I was exhausted when I finally reached Skarvheim. I was too excited about the good weather to be rational. If you're trying to save time, consider combining day 9 and 10 or days 17 and 18 - but note that any combination day means you'll be hiking a minimum of nine hours.

Krykjestølen is a tiny town - in fact, in Norwegian, it's called a "tettsted", which very roughly translates to "a place with some stuff that's too small to be a village"

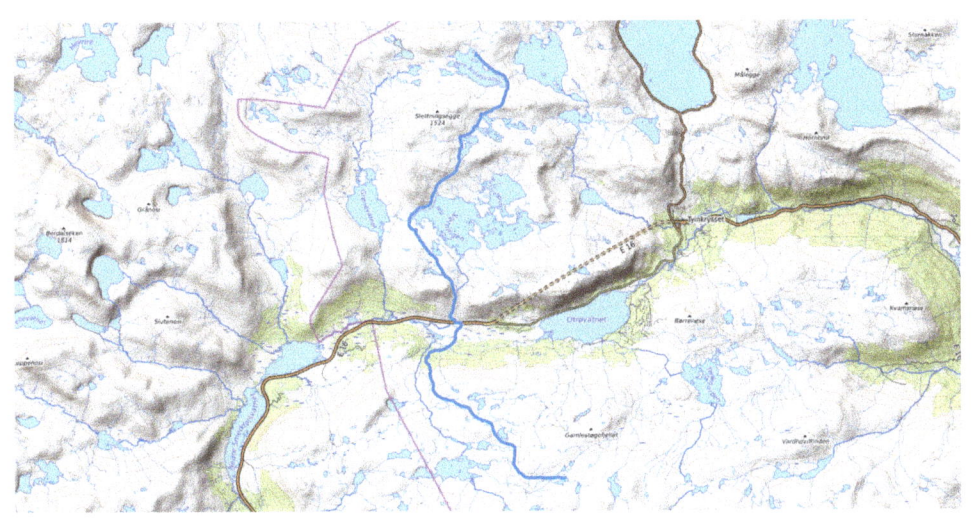

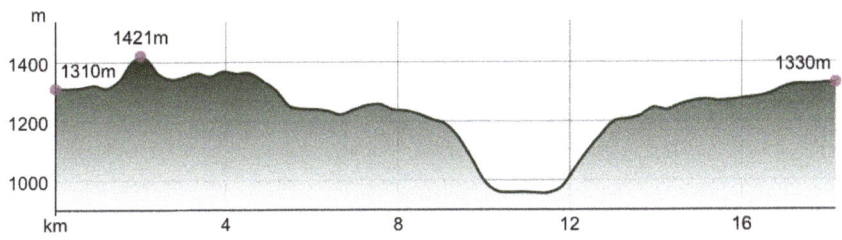

Sulebu - Skarvheim

| 19.0 km | 529 meters | 833 meters | 6 hours |
| 11.8 miles | 1,736 feet | 2,733 feet | Challenging |

This stage starts going around a small lake behind Sulebu, then up to the top of a bowl. It's rocky through this section, but not difficult to traverse. From here, you will go over a series of small ridges in a combination of dirt trails and rocks. With two kilometers left, the trail starts a very steep descent to Skarvheim. The descent is on a dirt trail that can be overgrown - be careful not to go too fast and slip in this part. You'll eventually reach the RV 52 highway, which you can cross to reach Breistølen Fjellstue, or turn left and hike up the road to Skarvheim.

My hiking notes

This is a relaxed hike in comparison to the days before. There's one tough climb up behind Sulebu, and then there are a series of small climbs and drops.

I mentally struggled with this section of the hike because I assumed that downhill would be faster than uphill. Given how steep it was, that was not the case. I should have trusted the UT times more and not assumed I could make up time.

If you want to stay at Breistølen Fjellstue, which is a traditional guesthouse, you need to book in advance. I didn't do that, so I ended up staying at Skarvheim, a self-service cabin that confusingly shares a name with the national park. (I had to repeatedly explain this to people who hadn't heard of the cabin.)

Skarvheim felt like a luxury hotel rather than a cabin to me - there was running water, a shower in a bathroom with heated floors, and even an electric kettle. The only challenge was that the gate was stuck shut and I had to hurdle over it.

m
1504m
1500
1333m
1300
1100
1051m
km
4
8
12
16

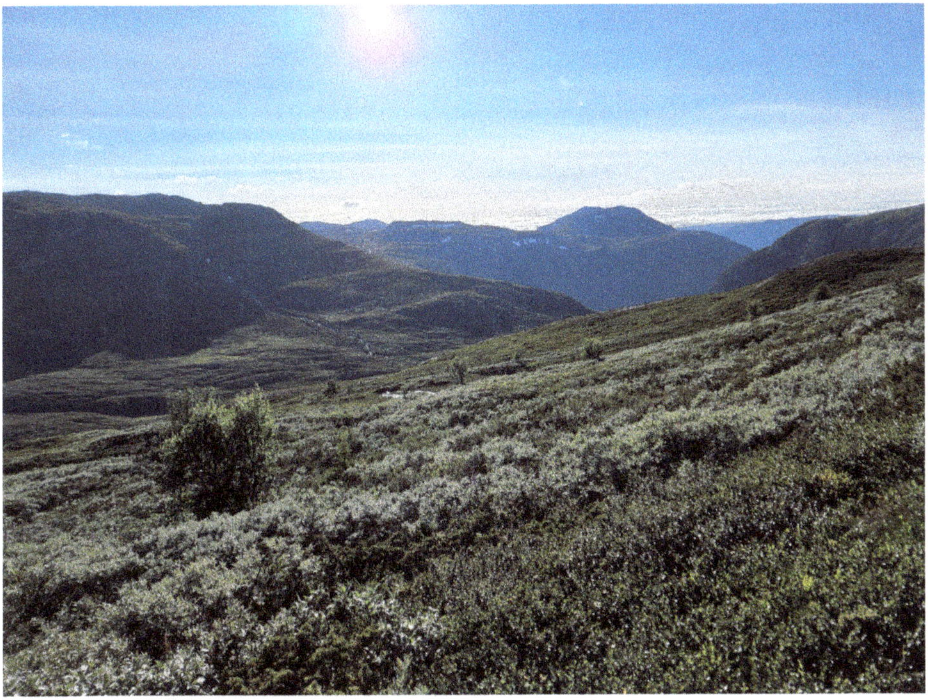

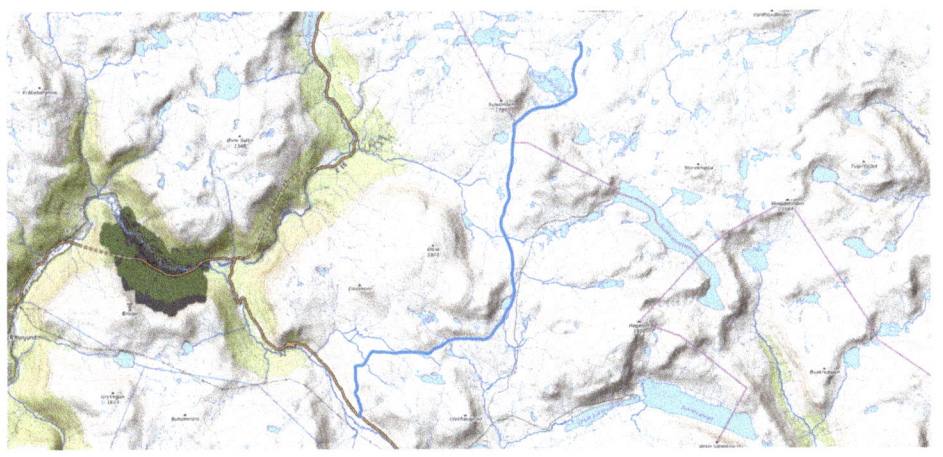

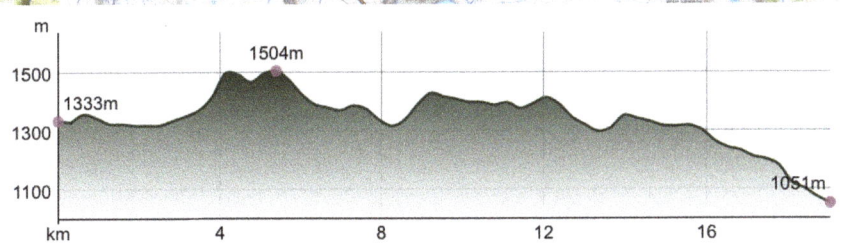

Skarvheim - Bjordalsbu

13.0 km
8.1 miles

613 meters
2,011 feet

104 meters
341 feet

5 hours
Challenging

Today's hike starts on a construction road, then further up a trail towards Stardalsmonen. The trail is easy and dirt in the morning. You'll gain elevation here, then gently drop elevation throughout the rest of the way. The trail passes the Starsjøen at 1,350 meters above sea level, then goes to the east of the Nedre Bjordalsvatnet before reaching Bjordalsbu.

Bjordalsbu is located at 1,580 meters along the Bjordalsvatnet (the Bjordals lake). As you get closer to the cabin, the trail gets rockier and rockier.

My hiking notes

The first kilometer had active construction work when I went up it, which wasn't a lot of fun. The trail was easy in the beginning of the day but got slower as I got closer to Bjordalsbu and started to go over rocks. The rocks in this section were definitely easier than the rocks in Breheimen at the beginning of the trail, but it was still a challenge to balance on them, especially with the backpack.

Bjordalsbu was a cool cabin - it was next to a small lake, and there was a sign on the door letting you know to close the door because of the beavers. It really feels like it's in the middle of nowhere, especially compared to Skarvheim the night before.

m
1565m
1500
1300
1100
1052m
km
3
6
9
12

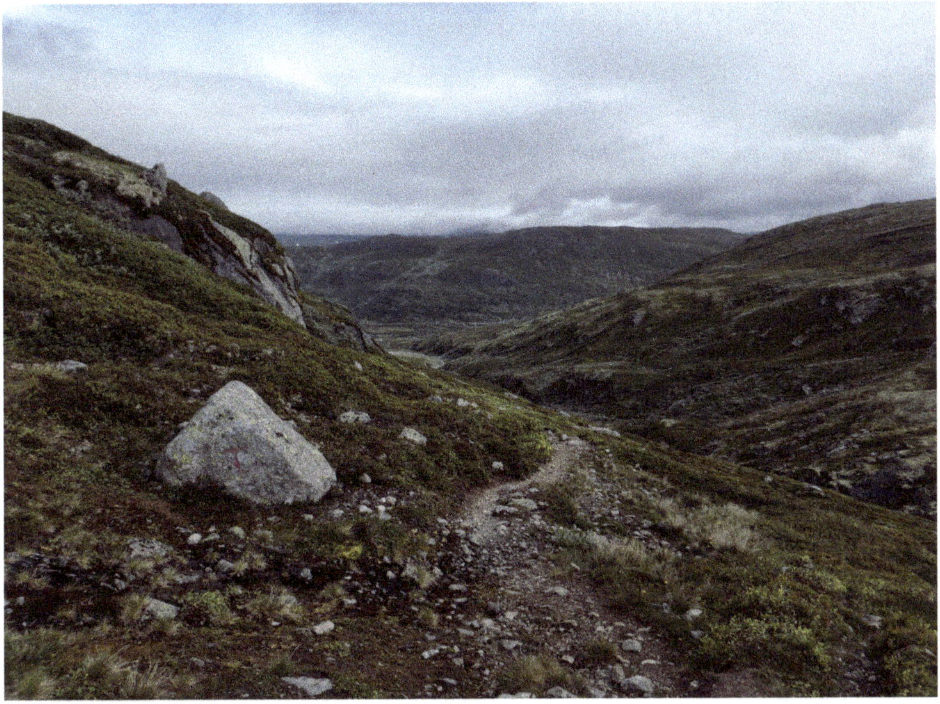

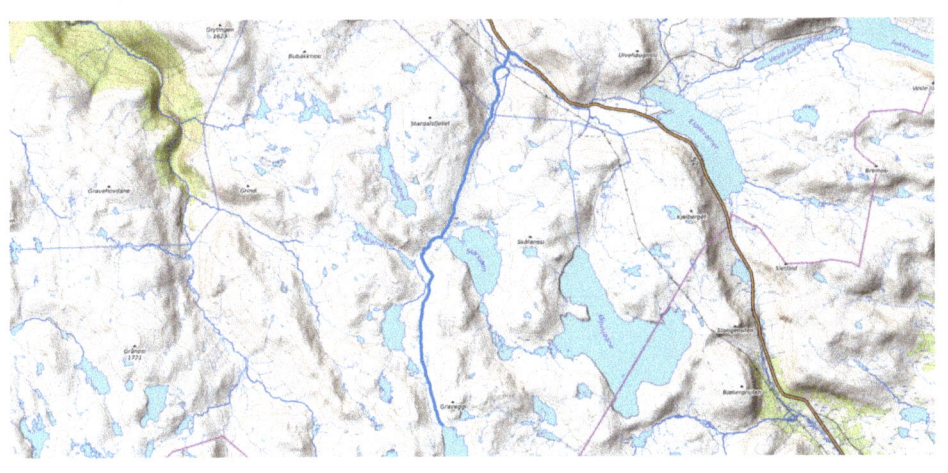

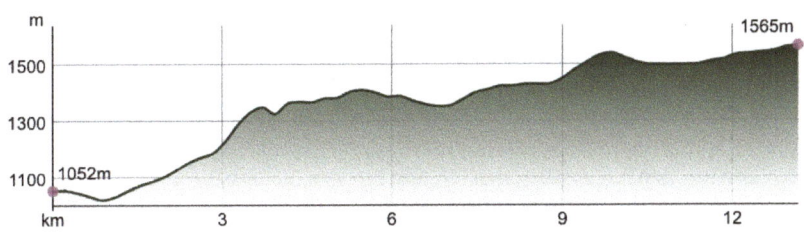

Bjordalsbu - Iungsdalshytta

| 16.0 km | 346 meters | 826 meters | 6 hours |
| 9.9 miles | 1,135 feet | 2,710 feet | Challenging |

Today's stage starts with rocky terrain around Bjordalsbu, gently gaining altitude as you get towards Skavlevatnet. You'll climb up to a ridge near Skavlevatnet, then start to drop elevation as you go towards Valevatnet. In this area, the trail starts to turn into a gentle dirt trail, and you'll rapidly drop elevation as you go towards Iungsdalshytta, with views out towards Fødalsvatnet and the surrounding mountains. Eventually, you'll drop down next to a waterfall that leads right to Iungsdalshytta, crossing a bridge and arriving at the cabin.

My hiking notes

I had a tougher time with this one than I expected. There were still snowfields on much of the rocky section, but I could hear running water underneath them and ended up having to detour to go around. I found poles super helpful on the snowfields and useless on the rocky section.

The trail got progressively easier during the day as I got closer to Iungsdalshytta. The trail crosses back into agricultural land, and I got very startled by a farmer who was setting up fences at one point.

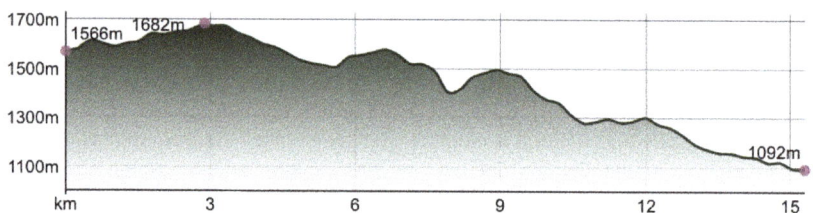

More sheep! I recommend filling up your water bottle in the first half of the hike to avoid drinking from streams in agricultural lands

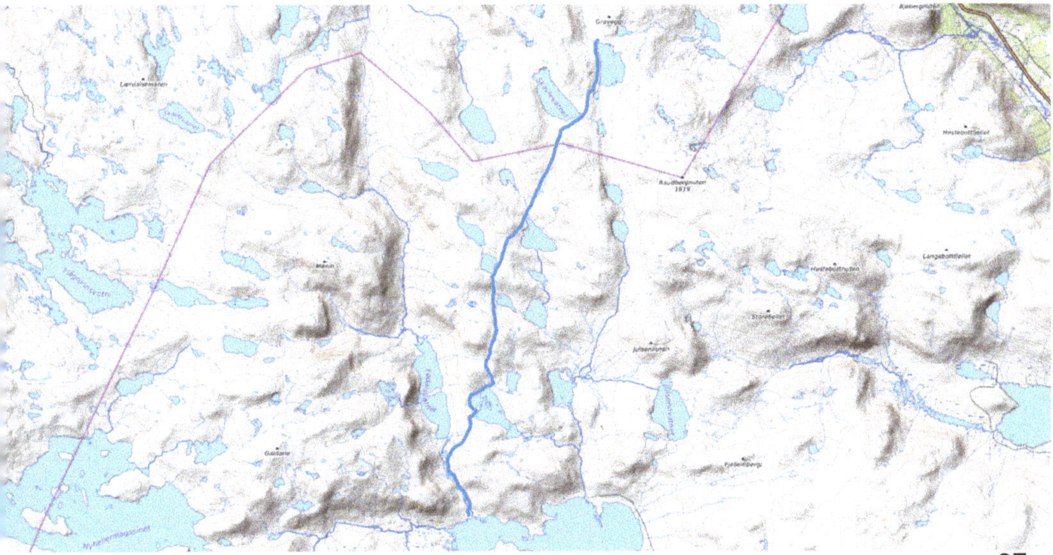

27

Iungsdalshytta - Kongshelleren - Geiterygghytta

| 28.9 km | 974 meters | 861 meters | 10 hours |
| 17.9 miles | 3,195 feet | 2,825 feet | Challenging |

This is the route's largest official day, although you can break it up by spending the night at Kongshelleren, a self-service cabin in the middle of the day. The day starts with a hike up through a bowl, starting with gentle elevation gain and increasing in difficulty as you get towards Kongshelleren. The path becomes rockier and rockier the closer you get to Kongshelleren as well. As you pass Kongshelleren after fifteen kilometers of hiking, the path changes back to dirt as you walk through meadows resembling that morning's section. Eventually, you will drop down to meet a construction road going towards Geiterygghytta. Follow it for a few hundred meters until you reach the cabin.

My hiking notes

The path is similar to the days before, although I thought it was rockier around Kongshelleren than it was around Bjordalsbu. It was difficult to find a lunch spot because of how rocky it was. As the day went on, the trail changed back to dirt and was easy to navigate.

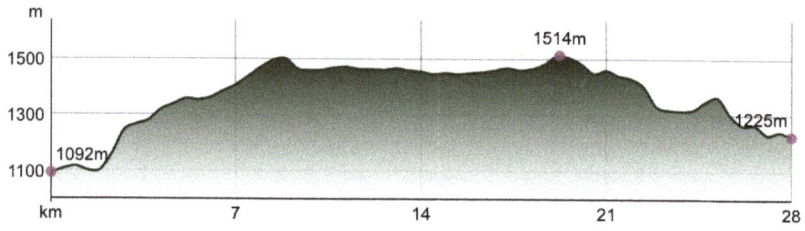

I'm really not sure why this is recommended as a single day rather than as two days - it's almost as long as combining the two days before. If you want to make it easier, spend the night at Kongshelleren. I'd recommend booking ahead there, since I heard from several people on the hike that it was completely full when they stayed there. Massiv has gotten much more popular, and Kongshelleren isn't a huge cabin.

Geiterygghytta - Finsehytta

16.1 km
10.0 miles

421 meters
1,380 feet

477 meters
1,564 feet

5.5 hours
Challenging

Today starts going along the Geiteryggvatnet (goat's back lake). The first section is flat and dirt paths, easy to follow. Eventually, you walk up the side of the bowl and onto a mountain plateau. This section has numerous snow fields that last even into the summer, and you will walk over snowfields and rocks. After seven to eight kilometers of total hiking, you will pass Klemsbu, a serving cabin that's only open in the winter but can be used for emergency shelter in case of bad weather. After this, you'll start to drop towards Finse, with views out onto the Finsevatnet and the glacier over Finse. Eventually, you'll reach the town and cross over the railroad tracks to reach Finsehytta.

<u>My hiking notes</u>

This was a special day for me because Finse was the first place in Norway that I went hiking. It's not really a town so much as a train station with some cabins around it, and there is no store to stock up on supplies in Finse. But it's a good drop point if you need anything, since the train goes back to civilization from here. Finsehytta feels more like a hotel than most of the cabins the night before, and it's one of the busiest in the entire DNT system.

The hike itself is pretty straightforward. There will likely be snowfields left near Klemsbu, so I recommend poles. The sticks that are in the snow from ski season tend to track the summer hiking trail accurately.

This photo shows Finse. All of Finse. It's not really a town, just a collection of cabins

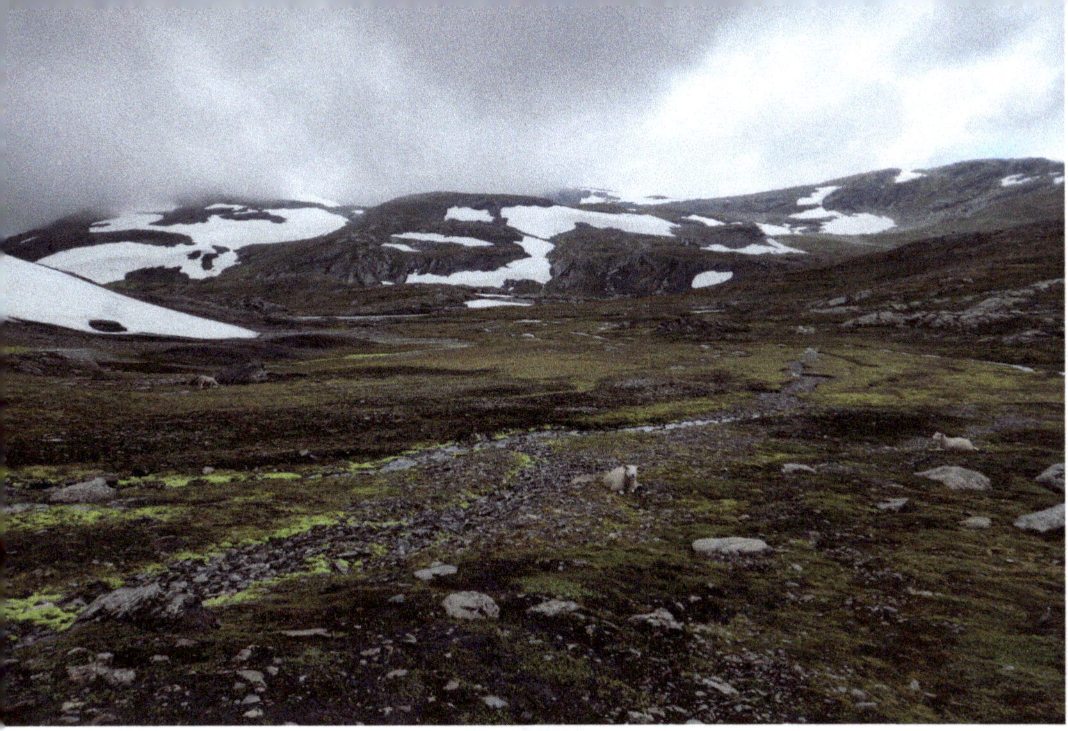

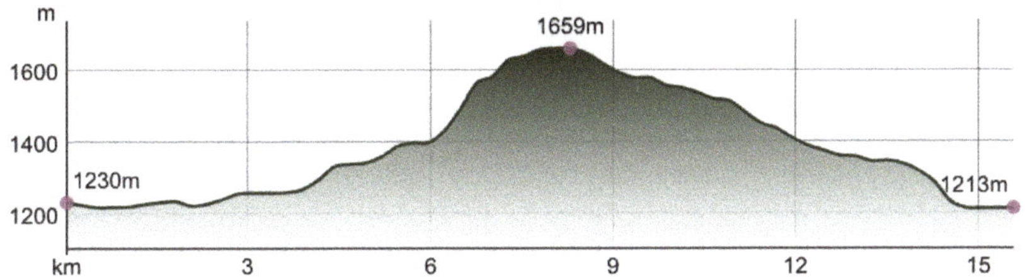
m
1600
1400
1200
1659m
1230m
1213m
km
3
6
9
12
15

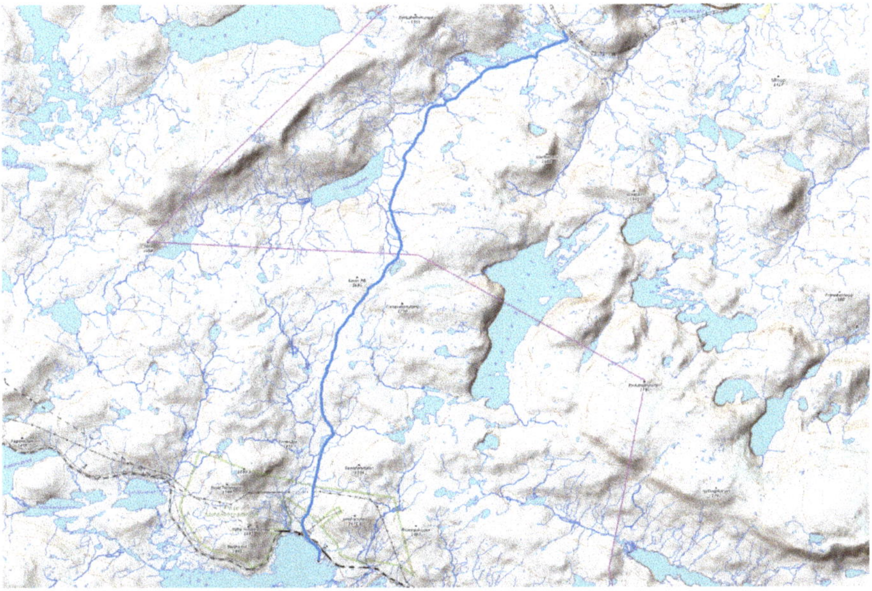

Finse - Krækkja

24.4 km
15.2 miles

797 meters
2,616 feet

843 meters
2,765 feet

8 hours
Challenging

Start the morning following the Rallarvegen, a biking trail, towards the Finse lake and then cross over the lake. This area can be buggy, so you may want to use bug spray or a mosquito net if you have it. After this, you'll start following a rocky trail by numerous small lakes, crossing a series of small summer bridges to get to Krækkja. The trail is substantially flatter than the earlier days, so you'll make good time even with the slightly rockier trail.

My hiking notes

Budget extra time to get through breakfast at Finse - it's a first cabin for a lot of visitors and doesn't always have the space for everyone to make breakfast. People are also heading out for bike trips to Flåm, so it can be bustling.

There were a lot of bugs near the Finse lake when I started, but they didn't bite as long as I kept moving. This was the first day where I really started to notice the change in landscapes from the beginning of the hike. It was rocky in the morning, but got progressively easier throughout the day.

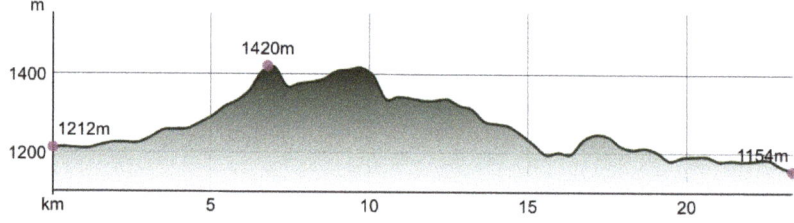

> *The climbs today feel much easier in comparison to the past few days - and definitely easier than the climbs at the start of Massiv*

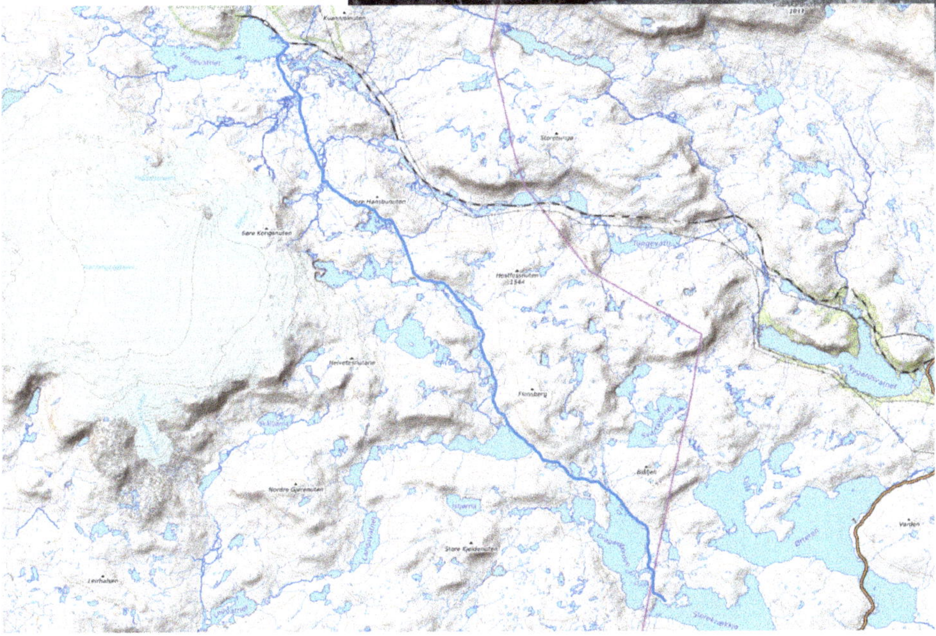

Krækkja - Stigstuv

20.0 km **12.4 miles**	**446 meters** **1,463 feet**	**366 meters** **1,201 feet**	**6 hours** **Challenging**

Start the morning retracting your steps from yesterday until you reach a sign showing the trail branching off towards Stigstuv. The trail is largely flat and dirt through this section. You will follow the trail to Halne, where you'll cross a road and then hike another 1-2 hours to reach Stigstuv.

<u>My hiking notes</u>

I actually thought the terrain in this section got a little boring - I prefer high peaks and bowls to the expansive vistas of the Hardangervidda, but it was impressive all the same. It's also a nice break for your feet after the days on the rocks. In retrospect, I wish that I had brought trail runners for this section to save my feet from having so many days in hiking boots.

The trail is a little bit difficult to spot near Halne, so check UT. I had to stop a few times to find it again.

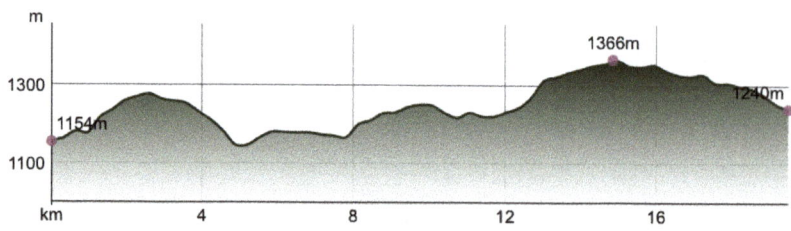

34

Stigstuv - Sandhaug

23.0 km	215 meters	203 meters	6 hours
14.3 miles	705 feet	666 feet	Challenging

From Stigstuv, start going west towards Sandhaug. The path is well-marked through this area, but be sure not to accidentally turn off onto one of the horse trails that cross the path. You'll continue in flat terrain until you can see a collection of cars at Tinnhylen in the distance. You'll hit a road, turn right, and hike up to Tinnhylen and a bridge to cross Tinnhølen. After this, continue following the trail southwest until you reach Sandhaug. The path is flat and easy to follow in this section.

My hiking notes

The trail was much more crowded that it had been the days before, and there were many more families in this section.

Sandhaug is located right in the middle of the route network for Hardangervidda, so if you're traveling with a group or during a popular time of year, you might want to book a bed in advance. It was one of the few cabins where I ended up sleeping in the dormitory rather than in a room.

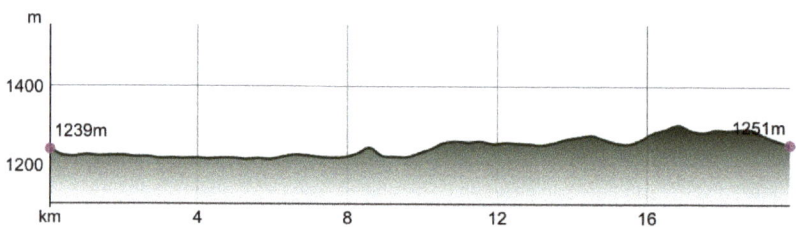

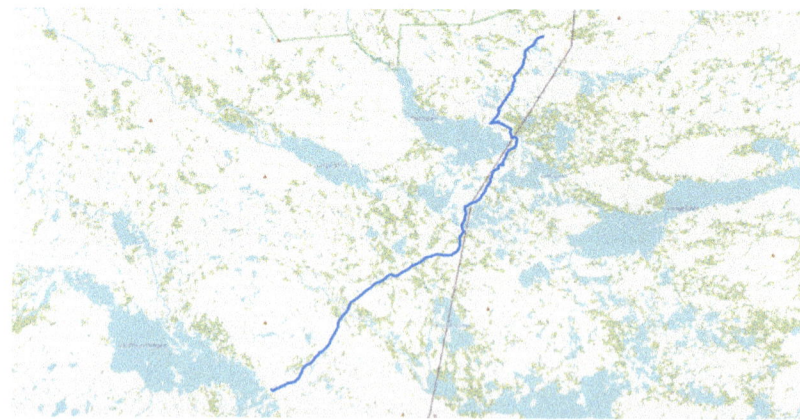

I thought Tinnhylen would have more shops or something, but it's just a giant parking lot. If you need anything from civilization, it's best to get it at Finse before you start the Hardangervidda. (Tinnhylen is in the picture to the right - as you can see, not much there)

Sandhaug - Litlos

| 25.6 km | 283 meters | 326 meters | 8 hours |
| 15.9 miles | 930 feet | 1,070 feet | Challenging |

Start today's hike going towards the south, over two summer bridges, then turn slightly to the west and continue hiking on the marked trail. This section has several summer bridges over rivers, and you will pass by many lakes, and likely people fishing into those lakes as well. You're very far from civilization now, but the trail is flatter and easy to hike through.

My hiking notes

The trail continued to be fast going today - it's flat and not rocky, and compared to the beginning of the hike, it's basically a walk in a park. (It's a national park, to be precise.) Despite how long the hike is today, it's very doable after you've conquered the first half. This is actually why I recommend doing Massiv from north to south - you build up so much hiking stamina and mental strength that way.

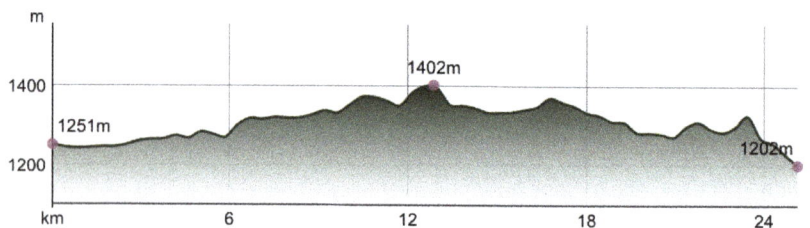

I loved Litlos as a cabin. It's very cozy and completely cut off from civilization. The only downside is that that means no phone service, either - Hardangervidda is a little bit light on the phone service. Check the weather forecast before you get there.

Litlos - Hellevassbu

| 16.0 km 9.9 miles | 469 meters 1,539 feet | 488 meters 1,601 feet | 5.5 hours Challenging |

Start today going west towards the river and then over a summer bridge. You'll follow the trail south along the Litlos lake, then continue along the trail, crossing a few small summer bridges as you get closer to Hellevassbu. The trail is mainly flat and dirt, although slightly rocky as you get closer and closer to Hellevassbu.

My hiking notes

This was straightforward hiking - lots of bridges to cross and a small climb, but it wasn't much compared to the beginning of the hike. The mountains around me felt much closer and taller than the days before. The day felt really short in comparison to the earlier hikes.

There's no service at Hellevassbu, so no way to check the weather.

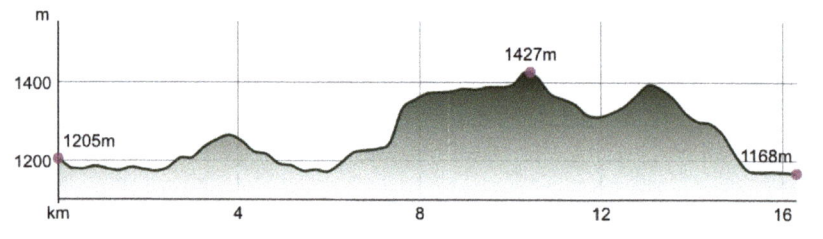

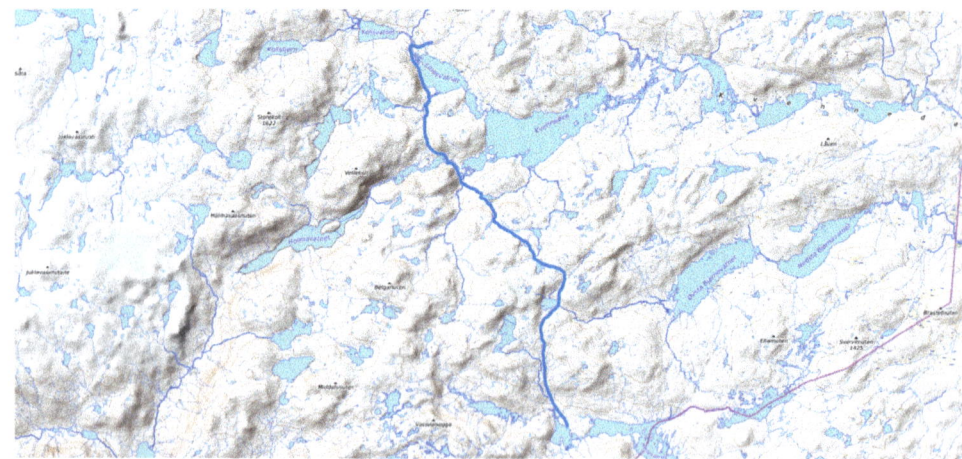

Hellevassbu - Haukeliseter

| 21.0 km | 565 meters | 763 meters | 7 hours |
| 13.0 miles | 1,854 feet | 2,503 feet | Challenging |

This is the last day of Massiv! The trail starts going south from Hellevassbu in easy to pass trails. You go by Helle lake, then up and down a series of small ridges. This area has more elevation change than I expected from the map, so be prepared. The last three kilometers are straight down as you cross a ridge then down towards Haukeliseter, eventually crossing the road and going to the last cabin on the journey. Haukeliseter is situated along a lake, looking south onto the mountains.

My hiking notes

This was an emotional bit for me. After 230 miles and 39,000 feet of elevation gain, more rain than I could measure, countless cabin friends made, and several liters of mountainside coffee, I was reaching the end. The Norwegian weather gods clearly knew it was the end of my journey, because I even had the sun break through the clouds as I crossed the last ridge to Haukeliseter.

Enjoy this one, and I hope that if you're reading this on the trail, you're damn proud of yourself.

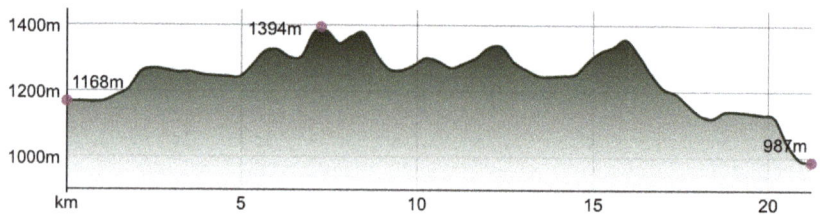

This is my "I did it!!!" face, crossing the last ridge to Haukeliseter

Route Extensions

If you're looking for ways to split up the hike or add more days to your hike, here are few ideas. You can do Massiv in sections over multiple years, and if you do that, you can add a few extra days to explore the national parks as you go.

Western route in Breheimen

This extension splits up the route from Sota Sæter to Nørdstedalseter into two additional days through western Breheimen. Breheimen is probably my favorite national park in Norway, with rugged peaks and dramatic waterfalls. It also splits up the first day of Massiv into shorter pieces (three 6 hour days rather than a 10-12 hour day).

Route	Length (km)	Elevation Gain (m)	Elevation Drop (m)	Time (ut. no)
Sota Sæter to Sprongdalshytta	18.2	741	217	6
Sprongdalshytta to Arentzbu	17.2	373	746	6
Arentzbu to Nørdstedalseter	15.7	748	688	6

A detour (en omvei) in Jotunheimen

This detour does a few of the final cabins of Omveien, a SignaTUR that goes from Lillehammer to the Sognefjord. Jotunheimen has the most alpine peaks of any place in Norway, so if you like the Alps, you'll like this extension.

Route	Length (km)	Elevation Gain (m)	Elevation Drop (m)	Time (ut. no)
Skogsdalsbøen to Leirvassbu	18.9	754	185	6
Leirvassbu to Olavsbu	10.6	363	327	3.5
Olavsbu to Fondsbu	13.8	335	716	5.5

Around the Hardangerjøkulen

The Hardangerjøkulen is the glacier behind Finse. This detour adds two days in between Finse and Krækkja as you go around the glacier rather than straight past it. It's not any easier than Massiv - these are intense, long days, but it's an undiscovered gem.

Route	Length (km)	Elevation Gain (m)	Elevation Drop (m)	Time (ut. no)
Finse to Rembesdalseter	20.8	429	695	8
Rembesdalseter to Kjeldebu	22.4	669	568	8
Kjeldebu to Krækkja	15.1	328	229	4.5

One way to Trolltunga

Trolltunga is one of Norway's most famous hikes and tourist attractions. If you want to see it but avoid the crowds in Otta, you can hike there from Tyssevassbu, a self-service cabin a day's hike away from Litlos.

Route	Length (km)	Elevation Gain (m)	Elevation Drop (m)	Time (ut.no)
Litlos to Tyssevassbu and Trolltunga *Stats are entire way from Litlos to Trolltunga. I recommend stopping at Tyssevassbu, doing a day trip to Trolltunga, and returning the day after to Litlos*	24.6	401	422	9

Western Breheimen Day 1: Sota Sæter to Sprongdalshytta

| 18.2 km | 741 meters | 217 meters | 6 hours |
| 11.3 miles | 2,431 feet | 712 feet | Challenging |

From Sota Sæter, you'll start by hiking along the road or the river to the parking lot near Mysubytta. I recommend going along the river over the road. It isn't much more elevation change, but it feels much more like the wilderness.

After that, you'll climb through a pine forest and then reach the turnoff for the trail towards Slæom. Turn towards the southwest and take the path towards Sprongdalshytta. The path will start climbing up gradually, passing by several small rivers and lakes. At about fifteen to sixteen kilometers, the path will get much more rocky and begin to climb much more steeply.

There are two to three kilometers of steep climb before the trail flattens out. From here, it's largely flat to Sprongdalshytta at 1,280 meters above sea level. Sprongdalshytta is a self-service cabin with a beautiful view out to the Jostedal glacier. It does not have phone service but fairly large. It was one of my favorite cabins to stay out, because it's nestled on a dramatic flat section - you have to cross a bridge over a lake to get to the bathroom from the main cabin.

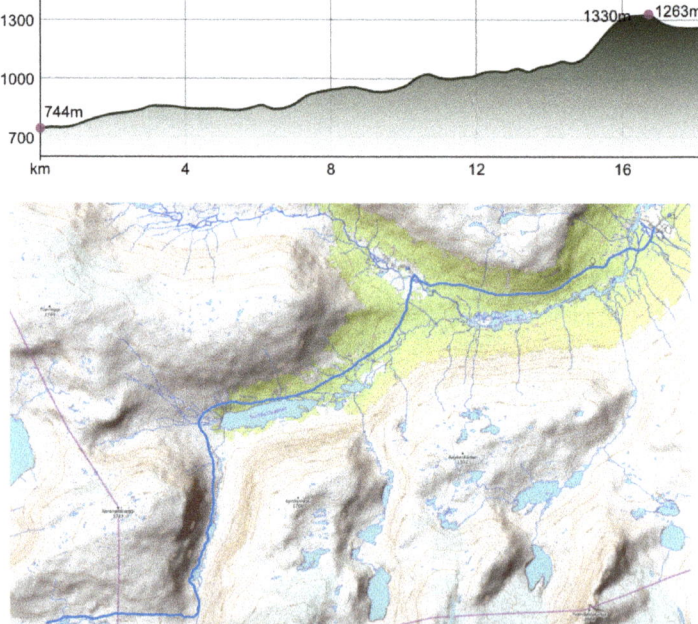

Western Breheimen Day 2: Sprongdalshytta to Arentzbu

17.2 km
10.7 miles

373 meters
1,224 feet

746 meters
2,448 feet

6 hours
Challenging

Follow the trail along the north side of the lake Sprongdalshytta sits on, then turn towards the south and take the trail towards Arentzbu. The day starts with a steep climb up to a saddle west of Greinbreen, the Grein glacier. This is a rocky climb, and it's really tough if it's been raining and the rocks are slippery. There are limited handholds and no chains to assist.

Keep climbing for about three kilometers until the trail reaches 1500 meters above sea level and a small lake. From here, the trail will start to drop back down, heading towards Arentzbu. This section is easier than the first part, but it's still technically tough. The trail goes over a few rivers that are usually walkable, but if there has been a lot of rain recently, they will need to be waded.

At the end of the day, the trail will pass the trail towards Nørdstedalseter, then turn west and end at Arentzbu. Arentzbu is a self-service cabin with no power or phone service, but it's nestled in a valley with gorgeous views.

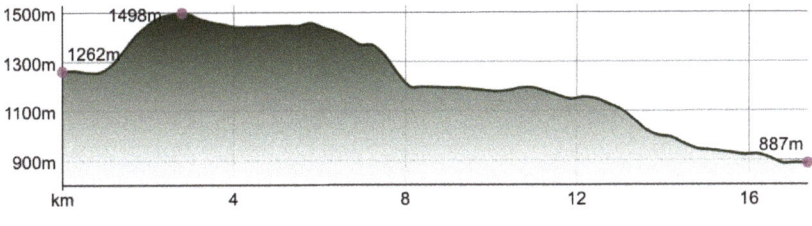

49

Western Breheimen Day 3: Arentzbu to Nørdstedalseter

15.7 km
9.8 miles

748 meters
2,454 feet

688 meters
2,257 feet

6 hours
Challenging

The day here starts out gently, then has a steep climb up Oksli. After climbing about 250 meters of elevation, the route turns further towards the east, and you'll continue towards Leirvatnet, where you can cross the river with a bridge. After the trail passes by Gravdalsvatnet, Gravdals lake, there's a steep downhill section on a trail. At the bottom of the trail, the trail meets up with a construction road, which it follows all the way to Nørdstedalseter.

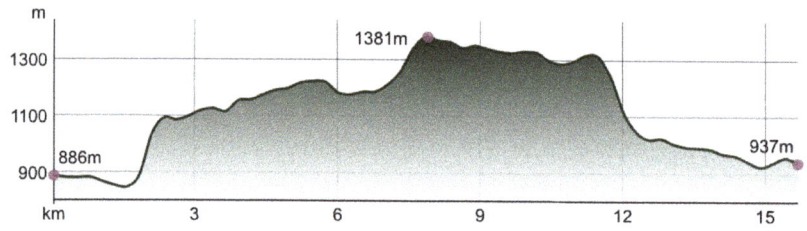

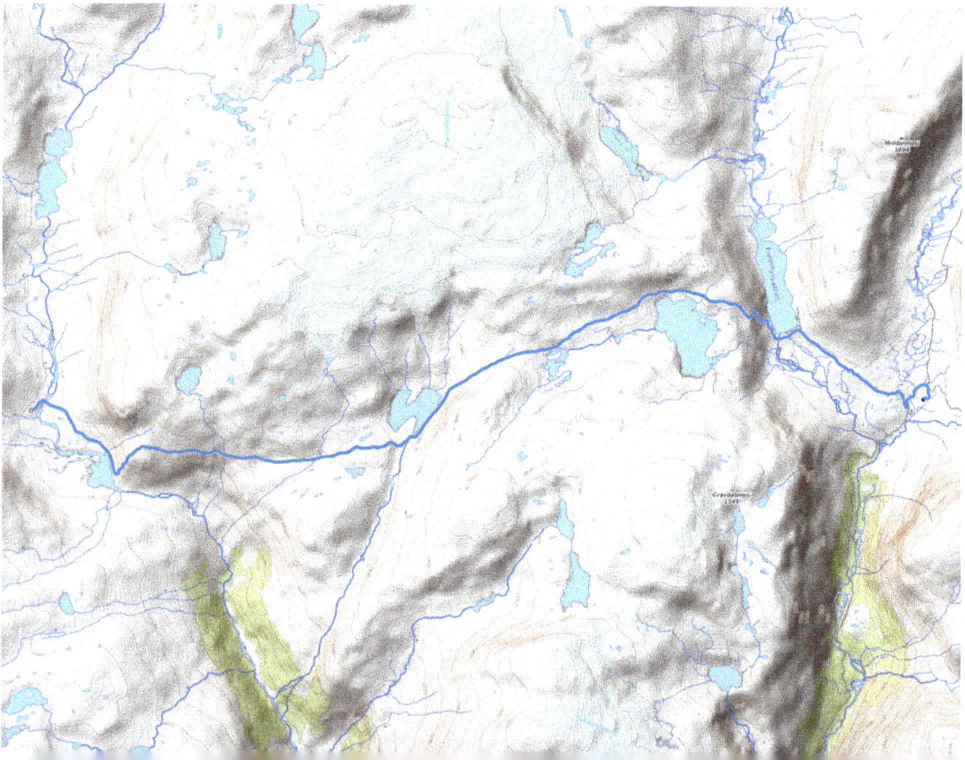

Omveien in Jotunheimen Day 1: Skogadalsbøen to Leirvassbu

18.9 km
11.7 miles

754 meters
2,474 feet

185 meters
607 feet

6 hours
Challenging

The route today starts by going north through the valley from Skogadalsbøen, past the meeting point with the trail coming down from Fannaråkhytta. From here, the trail turns towards the east and then starts to climb through the Storutladalen. The trail will start to come rocky through this section and continue to climb. Eventually, the trail passes by Gravdalsdammen and continues to climb in rocky terrain. At about eighteen kilometers in, the trail reaches an intersection with the trail coming from Olavsbu. Continue to follow the trail north for an additional kilometer to reach Leirvassbu.

Leirvassbu is a serviced cabin that was recently acquired by DNT. It's one of the busiest cabins in the DNT system and a favorite destination for people looking to explore the peaks in Jotunheimen.

It's also possible to skip Leirvassbu and go directly to Olavsbu from Skogadalsbøen if you're only looking to add one extra day to this detour. That route has less elevation change, so it takes about an hour less than the route to Leirvassbu.

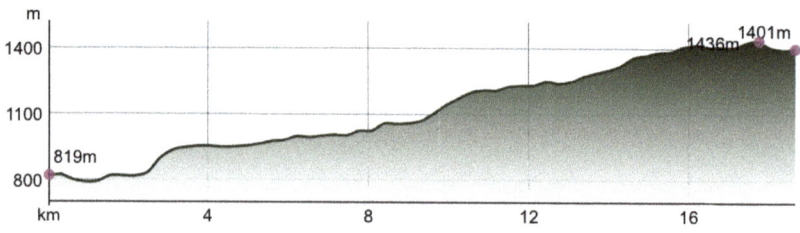

Omveien in Jotunheimen Day 2: Leirvassbu to Olavsbu

10.6 km
6.6 miles

363 meters
1,191 feet

327 meters
1,073 feet

3.5 hours
Moderate

In comparison to most of the days on Massiv, this is basically a rest day. The trail starts by going south from Leirvassbu, climbing slightly. The trail starts to drop a bit of elevation in rocky terrain, then continues on until it reaches the river coming from Nedre Høgvagltjønnen. It's usually possible to rock hop across the river here, but if there's been substantial rain, it will need to be waded. The path climbs a little bit more, going through a section where there can be snowfields until late in the summer. From here, it's a gradual drop to Olavsbu.

Olavsbu is DNT Oslo's largest self-service cabin. It can be a popular destination in the summer, so consider booking ahead.

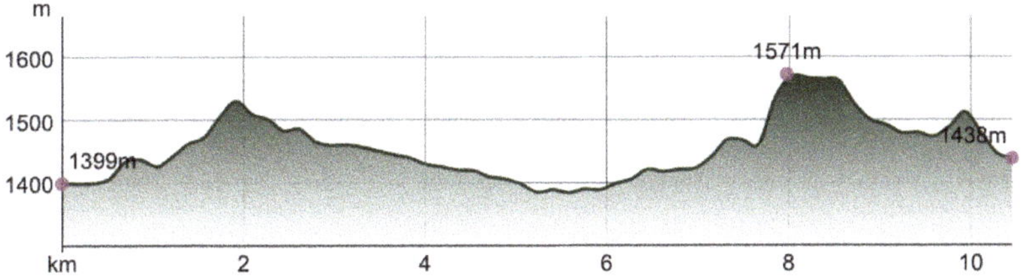

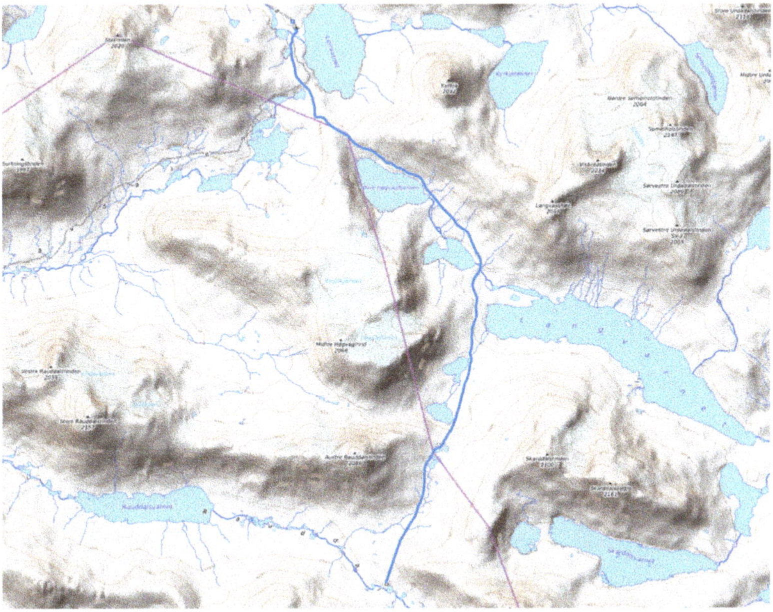

Omveien in Jotunheimen Day 3: Olavsbu to Fondsbu

13.8 km 8.6 miles	335 meters 1,099 feet	716 meters 2,349 feet	5.5 hours Challenging

Start by taking the trail towards Gjendebu for the first 1.5 kilometers of the hike. There is an old trail on the western side of the lake that is no longer in use. At about 1.5 kilometers in, cross in between two lakes and then start to take the trail towards the south. This section is flat and easy to hike.

From here, there's a short climb over a saddle, then a gradual drop down between Mjølkedalstinden and Snøhøltinden, two peaks ("-tinden" means "the peak"). Continue going south along the trail and pass the trails going to Gjendebu and Skogadalsbøen. From here, it's a steep descent down until you reach the cabins around Fondsbu. You can decide whether to take the road or one of the trails through the cabins to reach Fondsbu at the edge of

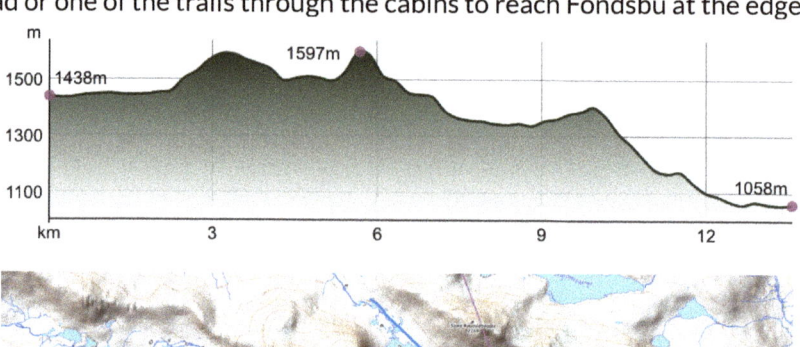

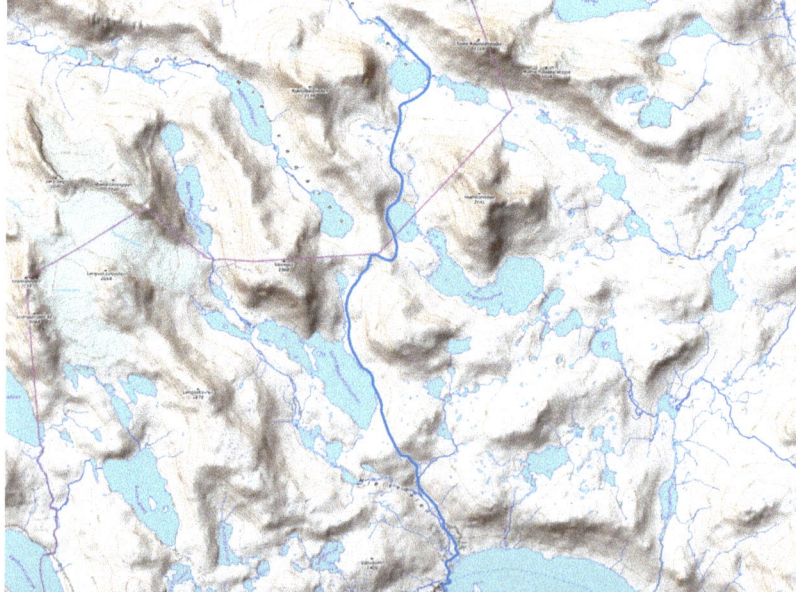

Around the Hardangerjøkulen Day 1: Finse to Rembesdalseter

| 20.8 km | 429 meters | 695 meters | 8 hours |
| 12.9 miles | 1,407 feet | 2,280 feet | Challenging |

This is a demanding route, although you'll get spectacular views of the glacier. If you're looking for an easier glacier experience, you can also do a guided walk on the Hardangerjøkulen leaving from Finse. (And if you're looking for an even easier day trip, you can bike to Hallingskeid and then take the train back.)

But if you're up for a more demanding route – the trail starts by going northwest from Finse, then turns towards the west. After about four kilometers of relatively flat trail, the trail starts climbing up to about 1,500 meters above sea level. Throughout this section, there can be snowfields left until the end of the hiking season, so bring and use poles if you have them. The snowfields can also obstruct the views of the cairns, so check frequently to make sure you're on the right path.

The trail curves and starts to head south again, running alongside two lakes. The path goes to the west of Luranuten, going past another small lake, then turns steeply downhill to reach Rembesdalseter at just over 900 meters of elevation.

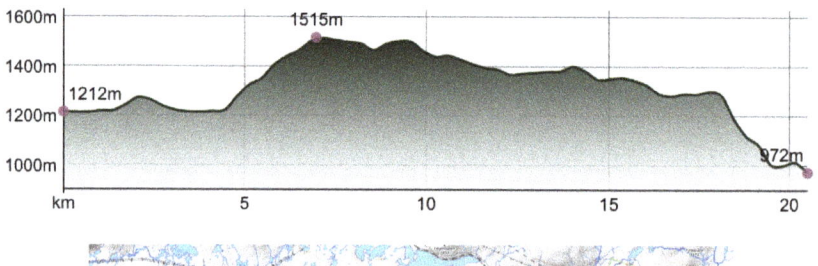

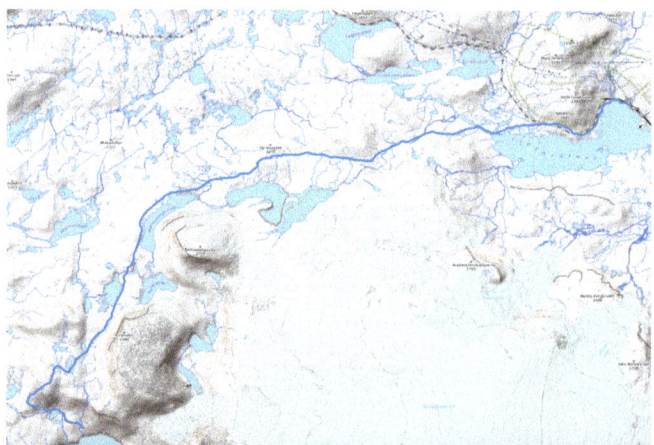

Around the Hardangerjøkulen Day 2: Rembesdalseter to Kjeldebu

22.4 km 13.9 miles	669 meters 2,195 feet	568 meters 1,864 feet	8 hours Challenging

The trail today starts by going to the southwest of the glacier. The trail climbs up to 1,300 meters above sea level, then starts to drop elevation through gently rolling terrain. There are several small rivers that the trail crosses, and some may need to be waded depending on the snow melt.

After about fourteen kilometers, the trail meets up with the trail to Kjeldebu heading towards the east. Turn onto this trail and follow it for an additional eight kilometers. This section gradually drops elevation and then flattens out, going abode the Sysenvatnet until it reaches Kjeldebu. Kjeldebu is a large self-service cabin, with more than 50 beds.

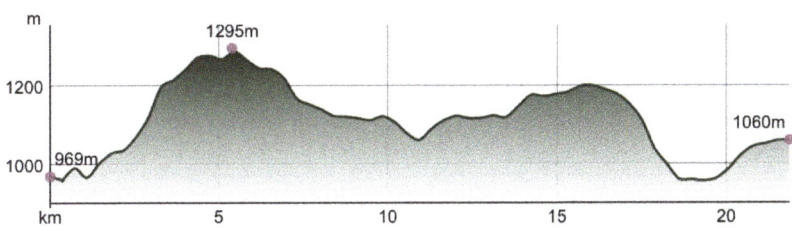

Around the Hardangerjøkulen Day 3: Kjeldebu to Krækkja

15.1 km
9.4 miles

328 meters
1,076 feet

229 meters
751 feet

4.5 hours
Moderate

The route starts by going to the northwest to go around the lake Kjeldebu is next to, then over a temporary bridge and along the north side of the water. From here, the trail continues going east with a gentle descent throughout the day. The trails are a mixture of rocky and dirt throughout the day, but there are plenty of spots to fill up a water bottle.

After 13 to 14 kilometers of hiking, the trail meets up with the trail coming from Halne. Turn towards the north and follow the trail for an additional kilometer until you reach Krækkja.

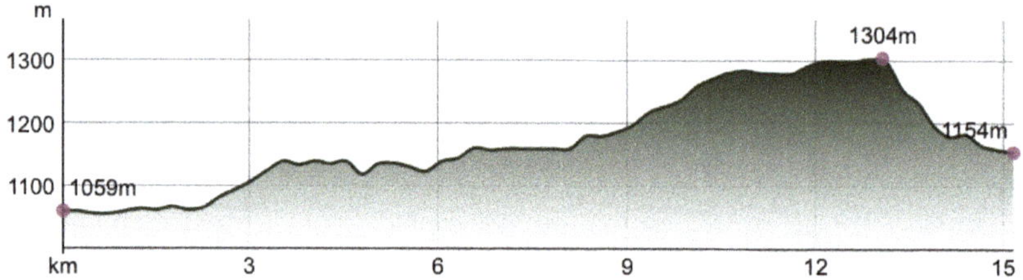

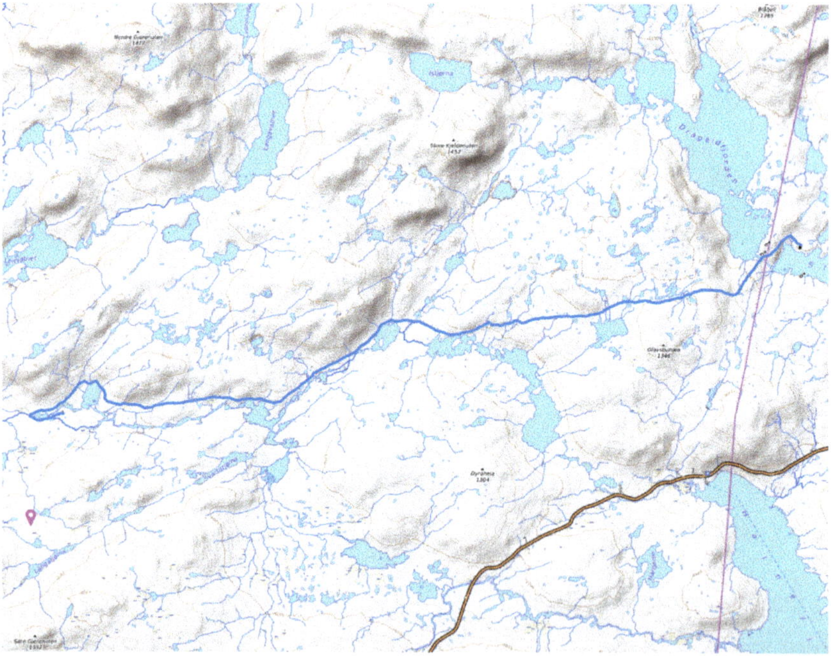

Litlos to Tyssevassbu and Trolltunga

24.6 km 15.3 miles	401 meters 1,316 feet	422 meters 1,385 feet	9 hours Very challenging

Trolltunga is one of the most famous hikes in Norway, and it's gotten very crowded in recent years with hikers who go up to Trolltunga from Otta. But it's also possible to get to Trolltunga from behind, starting at Tyssevassbu, a self-service DNT cabin. To do this extension, you hike from Litlos to Tyssevassbu, spend the night at Tyssevassbu, do a day trip to Trolltunga, and then head back to Litlos the next day.

The trail from Litlos to Tyssevassbu starts going west from the cabin alongside a lake, then continues to the west with a very gradual climb over the course of the day. The trail is a mixture of rocks and dirt. As the trail gets closer to Tyssevassbu, there may be snowfields left on the route.

The trail from Tyssevassbu to Trolltunga is not DNT maintained, so there are sections where the markings are worn away or hard to see. It follows the power line from Tyssevassbu to Trolltunga. The route is not recommended in poor weather, since it is exposed the whole way. In heavy rain or fog, it may not be possible to see all of the markings to follow to Trolltunga.

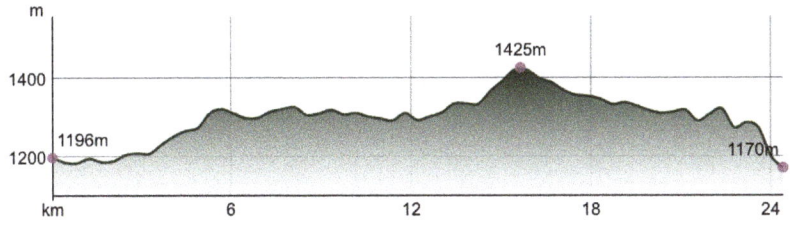

Logistics

Getting There and Back

There are only a few cabins in Massiv that are accessible via public transportation:

<u>Sota Sæter:</u> take the bus from Oslo to Otta or Lom. From here, you can transfer onto a bus to Dønfoss bru. During the summer season, the Dønfoss bru bus will drive all the way to Sota Sæter 3-4 times a week. If the bus doesn't drive all the way into the cabin, you'll have to call a taxi for the rest of the way. Call Skjåk taxi and arrange transport in advance - taxi companies may not answer on weekends or after hours.

<u>Sognefjellshytta:</u> buses to Sogndal / Lom (line 200) and Fortun / Gaupne (line 860) stop by the cabin once or twice a day. From Sogndal, you can fly to Bergen or Oslo. From Lom, there's bus service to either Oslo or Lillehammer.

<u>Fondsbu:</u> line 300 goes from Eidsbugarden next to Fondsbu to Tyinkrysset, where you can then transfer to buses that go to Oslo and Bergen. The bus runs twice a day.

<u>Skarvheim/Breistølen Fjellstue:</u> Bus line 170 to Oslo passes by Breistølen Fjellstue three times a day. It needs to be booked at least fifteen minutes prior to departure.

<u>Finse:</u> Finse is one of the easiest locations to get back to civilization from - the train between Bergen and Oslo stops at Finse approximately every two hours. It's the last easy drop point before you enter the Hardangervidda.

<u>Haukeliseter:</u> a bus line called the Haukeli Express runs in between Bergen and Oslo, stopping at Haukeliseter. It runs 3 times a day during the summer season.

To check bus times, use entur.no. Google Maps isn't accurate inside Norway and will not show all bus options.

If you need to get supplies while you're on the trail, there are limited options. Tyinkrysset, which you pass in between Fondsbu and Slettningsbu, has a small grocery store and sports store with limited hours. Otherwise, you'll need to either purchase what you need at a serviced cabin or take the bus back to civilization.

Timing

The cabins open in late June, so it's possible to start then, but I wouldn't recommend it. Given the amount of planning required for transit, I would recommend going in August. The chance that you have to reschedule the whole trip is much lower than in July, and all of the summer bridges will be up. There will also be many fewer snowfields left to cross. If you do need to go in late June or early July, check senorge.no before you go to see how much snow is left on the trail and plan accordingly.

Camping

Norway has some of the most permissive laws in the world around camping. Norway has a law called the Allemannsretten that guarantees the ability of people to explore and experience nature, even in privately owned areas, as long as you're in uncultivated land. Once you're in the wilderness, you may camp in any area, as long as you're at least 150 meters away from the nearest inhabited house or cabin. Note that the 150 meters applies to the DNT cabins as well - most serviced cabins have marked areas where you can camp, and you'll have to pay a small fee to use the toilets or other common facilities.

There are a few exceptions to this - notably, in Finse you are not allowed to camp on the north side of the lake, because that is used as the public water supply. There are signs up if there are camping restrictions.

Campfires are prohibited everywhere in Norway from April 15 to September 15. You will need to bring a gas stove to cook, and in the case of drought, even gas stoves may be banned.

It's more difficult to camp during the first half of the trip because the terrain is rocky, but the second half of the trip has tons of good camping spots. The people I met who were camping while doing Massiv were projecting to take 1-2 weeks beyond the standard time.

You can buy supplies at the self-service cabins by using the Hyttebetaling app, even if you're not spending the night at the cabin. Otherwise, there are very limited places along the trail to get supplies. The best way to get supplies is by taking the train to Geilo from Finse.

If you want to be added to the Hall of Fame, make sure to use SjekkUT on the UT app to check in at the cabins regardless.

Planning Resources

UT App and Checking In

In order to be added to the online Hall of Fame for Massiv, you'll need to check in on the UT app (which is sometimes referred to as "SjekkUT", or "check out") at the various cabins or landmarks that you stop at. The UT app only has instructions in Norwegian, so how to do that:

<u>Following a hike – needs to be done in advance:</u>

1. For starters, download the ut app. Once you've downloaded the app, make a profile with your email address and log in on your device.

2. From there, you have to follow the hikes that you want to take. Following the hikes will download the maps around the cabins or areas on that hike, so you'll be able to use them without internet service. This is important.

3. Adding the route to your account is not entirely intuitive. You will need to search for the name of the hike in the search bar. From here, the critical thing is that you follow the list, not the hike. It will be at the bottom of the search results.

4. Click on the list. Make sure it's the one with the list icon. If you click the three dots on the side, you'll get a button that says "Følge", or "follow." Click on that.

5. Congratulations! You have now followed the hike. The maps will download to your phone while you have service.

<u>Checking in:</u>

When you get to a cabin or landmark, you can check in. Click on the icon for the cabin or landmark on the map, and a little green button that says "SjekkUT" will show up on the bottom left. Click on it.

A new screen will pop up. Click on the green button at the bottom again. If you see a screen with confetti, you're checked in!

yr.no is the best resource for weather in Norway. It allows you to hike by specific cabin or mountaintop, with the weather for that particular point rather than the overall area. It's available in English.

Senorge.no shows the current and historic weather conditions for any point in Norway. It's very useful for checking the amount of snow remaining for summer hikes, as well as seeing if it's rained recently. Massiv often has snow into late in the summer season, and SeNorge will show you the latest snow cover reports.

Ut.no, both the app and website, is the best source of information on cabins and trails, as well as a great map of Norway. It's unfortunately only in Norwegian. You can download offline maps by going to "Profil" and then "Mine offline-kart" on the app.

Varsom.no is key for the winter and shows storm and avalanche warnings. It's available in English.

If you're stopping by a DNT office before going hiking, you can pick up a planleggingskart, or planning map. These aren't usable for hiking but are great for planning, since they show the locations of cabins and DNT cabins.

Packing List

Gear

☐   46-55 liter hiking backpack with a rain shield

☐   Maps and compass: *the maps in this guide are overview maps, and I strongly recommend getting 1:50,000 hiking maps just in case you're caught out in low visibility conditions or your phone battery dies.*

☐   Hiking poles: *they were super useful for long, flatter sections, snowfields, and river fording. I also used them to poke the ground to make sure it was real ground and not just mud*

☐   Duct tape

☐   Dry bags for packing: *I learned on day two that it can rain enough to soak through a rain shield and plastic bags. Rest in peace, laptop.*

☐   Vindsekk, or emergency bivvy: *especially if you're hiking early in the season*

☐   First aid kit

Clothing

☐   Hiking boots

☐   Trail runners: *these are optional, but they're great for the Hardangervidda. I didn't need my heavy hiking boots for the flatter, dirt sections there.*

☐   Rain pants and optional gaiters: *in myr or grasses, the water from plants nearby will soak into your pants if you don't have rain pants or gaiters.*

☐   Rain jacket

☐   Windbreaker: *it's frequently misting in the mornings, so if you don't like hiking in your rain jacket, bring a lighter weight jacket to hike in*

☐   Wool socks, two pairs: *I use one pair of socks for hiking and one pair for the cabin.*

☐   Hiking pants or long underwear to layer under rain pants

☐   Wool sweater

☐   Extra warm jacket

☐   Two sports bras and two pairs of underwear

☐   Hat and gloves

☐   Two hiking shirts

Cabin Supplies

☐ Mini towel: *for cabins with showers. The showers are usually single gender but communal, so the towel is handy even if you want to create a little shield to get changed under.*

☐ DNT key

☐ Sengetøy (sheet set) or sleep liner: *required for the cabins*

☐ Toilet shoes: *about half of the cabins have outdoor toilet, and this keeps you from having to put potentially wet hiking boots back on*

☐ Sleep mask: *there are good curtains in the cabins, but it never gets dark*

Food and Drink

☐ Thermos for hot drinks

☐ Small plastic water bottle: *there are plenty of rivers and streams to fill up a water bottle as you're hiking*

☐ Candy and snacks

☐ Plastic bag for sandwiches

Tech

☐ Phone: *I recommend downloading UT, YR, and Hyttebetaling before your hike*

☐ Battery pack: *almost all of the cabins have power, but there are limited outlets available. The battery pack is a good backup*

☐ Chargers: *many of the self-service cabins only have USB classic charging outlets. If you have a phone with a USB-C charging port, you will want to bring a USB to USB-C charger.*

Other

☐ ID and credit cards: *all of the cabins are payable with either credit card or the Hyttebetaling app, so there's no need to bring cash*

☐ Sunglasses and sunscreen: *the entire hike is unshaded, so if it's sunny, you'll need sunscreen*

☐ Toiletries - wilderness wash, face wash, toothpaste, toothbrush, contacts, contact lens solution, glasses, hairbrush, hair ties, nail clippers, any medications you take as needed

☐ Tiny shovel and toilet paper

☐ Extra plastic bags

Some Handy Norwegian Words

Almost all Norwegians speak perfect English. That said, there are times where it's handy to be able to read signs, the weather, or the map.

Hiking and the map

Bratt/meget bratt: steep/very steep

Breen: the glacier

Dalen: the valley

Grusvei: a gravel path

Luftig: steep drop offs on the side of the trail

Kvistet: marked (used for ski trails)

Merket: marked (used for summer trails)

Mobildekning: phone service

Myr: a swampy, wet land covering

Nord, sor, ost, vest: north, south, east, west

Skog: forest

Stein: rocky

Steinur: rocky patches to hike over

Tind/tinden: peak

Vadested: a place that requires wading

Vannet: the water

Varder: cairns

Vatnet: the lake

Vegen: road

Weather

Bris: breeze

Flom: flood

Lettskyet: barely cloudy

Lyn: lighting

Nedbør: precipitation

Nysnø: new snow (no icy cover yet)

Regn: rain

Weather continued

Skyet: cloudy

Snø: snow

Sol: sun

Soloppgang, solnedgang: sunrise, sunset

Strynregen: very heavy rain

Tåkete: foggy

Torden: thunder

Things in provision rooms

Bønnemix: mixed beans

Erter: peas

Fullkorn: whole grain

Gryte: stew

Hermetikk: shelf-stable boxes

Kaffe: coffee

Kanel: cinnamon

Kokemalt: coffee that needs to be cooked in a kettle

Kjeks: biscuits

Kjøtt: meat

Knekkebrød: crispbread

Kokk uten lokk: cook without a lid

Kylling: chicken

Lapskaus: a Norwegian stew of potatoes and meat

Legg til: add to (e.g. "legg til vann" = "add water")

Linser: lentils

Melkepulver: milk powder (reconstitute with water)

Ost: cheese

Pannekake: pancakes

Food continued

Potetmos: mashed potatoes

Rein: reindeer

Ror godt: stir well

Smør: butter

Sodd: a high calorie stew of pork, potatoes, and some vegetables

Sukker: sugar

Svine: pork

Syltetøy: jam

Turmat: dehydrated hiking food

Vann: water

Cabins

Betjent: serviced (a lodge)

Selvbetjent: self-service (a cabin without staff but with a provision room)

Ubetjent: unserviced (a cabin with beds, propane, and wood, but no food)

Drikkevann: drinking water

Forhåndsbestilt: booked in advance

Hyttefelt: a collection of cabins

Protokoll: the book you have to sign when you arrive at a cabin

Using the Cabins

One of the most amazing things about hiking in Norway is the national cabin network. The Norwegian Trekking Association (DNT) maintains a network of more than 600 cabins spread across the country. It makes it easy to travel deep into the wilderness without carrying food or a tent.

Cabins come in three grades:

Betjent (serviced):

These aren't cabins but full lodges. You'll have a three course meal for dinner, a buffet breakfast with a place to fill your thermos, showers and drying rooms for clothes, and often indoor toilets.

Dinners are served family style, where the staff will bring out giant tureens of soup for a first course, then usually some kind of meat and potatoes, then individual desserts. There's more than enough food for everyone - but make sure to book ahead and alert the cabin if you have dietary restrictions.

The family style dinners mean that you have to go to an assigned dinner time, usually seven o'clock. There's usually assigned seating. People are generally super friendly at dinner and chat about where you've hiked from that day.

Serviced cabins have electricity, but the number of outlets varies. At many cabins, there are only outlets in the common areas. At others, the electricity is turned off after dinner service ends, so don't rely on an overnight charge for your devices.

Serviced cabins also have drying rooms and showers (with the exception of Fannårken). Drying rooms usually have strong heaters and dehumidifiers that dry out gear overnight. Showers are usually communal for each gender, so if you're shy, try to go at an off-time.

You'll pack lunch for the next day at breakfast. There is parchment paper and sometimes plastic bags for taking sandwiches in - the Norwegians are generally happy to show you how to wrap a sandwich in parchment paper if you need help. The stay at an serviced cabin also includes a thermos fill up for the next morning - they'll let you know at check in if you should leave your thermos at the reception desk or bring it to breakfast to fill it yourself.

Selvbetjent (self-service)

Self-service cabins are unique to Norway. They're generally smaller than staffed cabins, but come fully stocked with a provisions room, wood for the fireplace, gas for cooking, and cooking supplies. Some have electricity, but it's usually from a single solar panel and is only enough to charge one or two phones. You usually have to fetch and boil water from a nearby water source.

The self-service cabins run on the honor system. They can be unlocked with the DNT key, which you can purchase at a DNT store in Norway, online at their web store ahead of the hike, or at a staffed cabin. To pay for your stay, use the Hyttebetaling app. The app allows you to keep a list of all the supplies you've used and then pay with credit card when you get back into phone service. The app is available in English.

Ubetjent (unserviced)

These are just like self-service cabins, except that there isn't food available in the provision room. There are no ubetjent cabins on the Massiv route.

Cabin Etiquette:

When you arrive at an unserviced or self-service cabin, the first thing to do is to unlock the cabin and then take off your shoes. No outdoor shoes are allowed in the cabin to help keep it clean. After that, fill in your information in the besøksprotokoll, a horizontal blue book that asks where you came from, where you're going, and your membership information. After that, you have the right to use the cabin. I generally first start a fire if the cabin is cold, then fetch water to heat up for dinner.

When you leave the cabin in the morning, you'll need to clean up. That means washing all of the dishes, cleaning out the ashes in the fireplace, bringing in fresh wood for the fire, washing the floors in the bedroom and common areas, and any other tidying.

You can use the cabins if you're camping. You'll need to register in the besøksprotokoll and pay for a day visit ("dagsbesøk"). After that, you can cook food or just relax for a bit. Make sure to sweep up and wash the floors after yourself.

Cabin FAQs:

It's not necessary to book in advance for the cabins - if you arrive at the cabin, you'll have a place to sleep, though it might be on a mattress on the floor if it's really busy. I generally don't book cabins in advance so that I have the most flexibility possible to change hiking plans based on the weather.

The exceptions to this are Fannaråkhytta and Kongshelleren (if you decide to split up the Geiterygghytta/Iungsdalshytta hike). Fannaråkhytta has to be booked in advance because it has very limited bed space and no floor space to put out mattresses on. Kongshelleren is a relatively small cabin that has become much more popular as Massiv has grown in popularity, and it has had several nights over capacity in the last few summers.

The other big exception – book ahead at the serviced cabins if you have dietary restrictions. Because meals are served family style, the cabins need advance notice to be able to accommodate dietary restrictions.

Joining DNT:

You should absolutely join DNT before starting Massiv - the savings on staying in the cabin will cover the cost of the membership in two to three nights. If you are planning to camp, you will still want to join DNT to get a DNT key. You'll need the key if you want to do a day visit or if you end up staying in a cabin during a day with particularly bad weather.

Joining online is a little confusing, and there are updated instructions on the blog. You can also stop by any DNT office in Norway.

Cooking at the cabin:

There is a propane stove and plenty of cooking supplies in the cabins. The food that you'll generally find breaks down into four categories:

Breakfast: knekkebrød (crispbread), oatmeal, pancake mix, leverposti (liver spread), jam and chocolate spread, mackerel in tomatoes , butter, jam, and honey

Dinner: fish soup, peas and carrots, mashed potato mix, lapskaus, rice, bacalo, boxed mixes for pasta and stews, pasta, reindeer meatballs, dry red lentils, and crushed tomatoes

Snacks and dessert: chocolate pudding, vanilla sauce, canned fruit in syrup, and biscuits/cookies

Misc things: dried hiking food, coffee, tea, hot chocolate, currant drink mix, hiking snacks like knekkebrød sandwiches, sugar, cinnamon

Each cabin has a different selection of food, and if you're late in the season, certain items might be eaten up. If you're vegetarian or gluten-free, make sure to have your own backup food.

My challenge with cooking at self-service cabins is finding something to bring for lunch the next day. I really load up on breakfast, often mixing vanilla sauce or jam into my oatmeal for the extra calories. I take two or three packages of freeze dried food with me to eat on the trail, in case there isn't shelf-stable cheese and knekkebrød for lunch.

Cabin Overview

Cabin	Cabin Type	Beds	Pre-bookable beds	Power
Sota Sæter	Serviced	86	86	Y - 220 volt
Nørdstedalseter	Serviced	42	42	Y - 12 volt
Sognefjellshytta	Private hotel	80	80	Y - 220 volt
Fannaråkhytta	Serviced	34	34	No
Skogadalsbøen	Serviced	87	87	Y - 220 volt
Fondsbu	Serviced	100	100	Y - 220 volt
Slettningsbu	Self-service	14	4	No
Sulebu	Self-service	22	12	Y - 12 volt
Skarvheim	Self-service	9	3	Y - 220 volt
Breistølen Fjellstue	Private hotel	20	20	Y - 220 volt
Bjordalsbu	Self-service	24	10	Y - 12 volt
Iungsdalshytta	Serviced	52	52	Y - 220 volt
Kongshelleren	Self-service	12	4	No
Geiterygghytta	Serviced	88	88	Y - 220 volt
Finsehytta	Serviced	174	174	Y - 220 volt
Krækkja	Serviced	85	85	Y - 220 volt
Stigstuv	Private hotel	30	30	Y - 220 volt
Sandhaug	Serviced	80	80	Y - 220 volt
Litlos	Serviced	52	52	Y - 220 volt
Hellevassbu	Self-service	24	9	Y - 12 volt
Haukeliseter	Serviced	174	174	Y - 220 volt

Phone Service	Drying Room	Shower	Drop point?	Other Notes
Y	Y	Y	Yes - bus and taxi	
N	Y	Y	No	
Y	Y	Y	Yes - infrequent bus (twice daily) to Lom	
N	Y	N	No	Must be booked in advance (limited number of beds)
N	Y	Y	No	
Y	Y	Y	Yes - bus service or boat to Bygdin	
N	N	N	No	
N	N	N	No	
Y	N	Y	Yes - bus service	
Y	N	Y	Yes - bus service	
N	N	N	No	
N	Y	Y	No	
N	N	N	No	Can become crowded; book in advance
N	Y	Y	Yes - bus to train station	
Y	Y	Y	Yes - train to Bergen or Oslo	
Y	Y	Y	No	
Y	Y	Y	No	
N	Y	Y	No	
N	Y	Y	No	
N	N	N	No	
Y	Y	Y	Yes - bus to Bergen or Oslo	

Massiv FAQs

Can I drink the water underway? Do I need to bring a water filter?
You can drink water directly from streams in Norwegian national parks. The cabins also have places where you can fill up water bottles, so no need to bring a water filter.

Where can I leave luggage?
If you have luggage or items that you don't want to bring on the hike, the best place to leave them is at the Oslo airport or train station. Officially, the luggage lockers can only be used for seven days, but it's possible to leave items for longer as well. Email hittegods.osl@no.issworld.com for the airport or oppbevaring@banenor.no for the train station, and let them know your locker number and plans.

Can you section hike the trail?
Yes, absolutely! Many of the Norwegians who do the trail plan to do it over multiple years. The sections split easily by national park. You can also pick any two cabins with public transit links (see the "How to Get There" section) and just do that section.

Am I okay just speaking English?
Absolutely. In my entire time in Norway, I have met only three people who couldn't speak English. The only challenge is that the labels on food in the self-service cabins are only in Norwegian. I've included some key words in the book for reading food labels.

How technical is the glacier crossing?
Not very. You'll be fine with regular hiking boots as long as you have layers to keep warm. The guides bring crampons for the group that enable you to walk over the ice, as well as the harnesses and rope for the group to go together.

Is it expensive?
It's about $100/night to stay in a serviced cabin, which includes all food, and $30/night to stay in a self-service cabin. It's a lot cheaper than other hiking trips I've taken because you don't have to pay for a hotel room - you pay by person rather than room. If you want to save on the cost, you can camp some nights rather than staying in the cabins.

Can I do laundry along the way?
You can hand wash clothes at the serviced cabins and then dry them in the drying room, but that's it. There are no laundry facilities.

Can I rely on the self-service cabins to have food and supplies?
Yes - I've visited 81 DNT cabins so far and have yet to find one that wasn't stocked. If you have dietary restrictions, though, make sure to bring some backup food. There is always food, but it is not always what you're craving.

How hard is navigation?

It's not bad at all - the trails are generally really well marked with the characteristic red T and very visible cairns. I used my phone rather than a map and compass. The UT app was a huge help.

That being said, I took maps and compass in case my phone died – that turned out to be a good move, because during really heavy rain, my phone got so wet that it stopped being able to sense touches on the screen.

Can I go from south to north on the trail instead?

Definitely, although I recommend going north to south so that you can do the toughest section on fresh legs. There's also a higher destiny of drop points in the northern section, so it's easier to get back to civilization if you want to stop the trail or need supplies.

Will I have phone service?

I've listed which cabins have phone service in the cabin amenity section, but generally, you should expect to have phone service for about half of the hike. Phone service generally varies during the course of the day - even if two cabins both have phone service, the hike in between them may not.

Are there bugs?

The only time I had bugs was around the lake near Finse. That being said, it was usually windy and cold enough that it wasn't good weather for bugs anyway. If you're sensitive to bugs, consider bringing a small thing of bug spray.

Why Massiv

A short personal note:

I discovered the Massiv trail while looking for trip ideas in summer 2015. I ended up on the Norwegian Trekking Association website, reading about Massiv via Google Translate. It was the most intense hike I'd ever seen.

And to be honest, it scared me. Cabins with people I didn't know, in a country where I didn't speak the language? Carrying all my stuff with me? And it was spectacular but technically challenging terrain.

Everything about this hike seemed too intense for me. A voice in the back of my head told me that maybe this was the kind of hike where I should know my limits. But something about the challenge excited me at the same time it terrified me, and Massiv became my bucket list hike.

It took until summer 2022 for me to actually start. It didn't start on a promising note - it was Norway's wettest summer in many years, and I had absolutely terrible weather for the first half of the hike. The initial days were often a slog to get through.

I have a scar on my leg from the second day. The second day is the toughest day of the entire hike. And the day I did it also happened to be the single worst weather day I've had in Norway. I had rain, snow, hail, freezing fog, and freezing rain. The trail flooded, and I was scrambling over rocks.

Two-thirds of the way through, I slipped on a rock and crashed forward, my entire weight landing on my shin. The landing was hard enough that I tore my rain pants completely open. But I was still ten or fifteen kilometers from Sognefjellshytta. It was a moment where I was literally lying on the ground, miserable, having failed. And I got up and kept going. I pushed myself up, readjusted my backpack, and kept walking.

The cut on my leg fortunately never got infected, but it never completely healed. I still have an inch long, bright red scar from where my shin made contact with the rock on the way now. I carry that scar now like a constant reminder. It's my version of a tattoo. On the physically toughest day of my life, I picked myself up and tried again.

What Massiv gave me was confidence in myself. I printed out the picture I took of myself crossing the ridge to Haukeliseter and hung it next to my desk, a reminder of how strong I am and that I can do anything I set my mind to.

Doing Massiv is worth it for the views alone. But I hope that it imbues you, too, with the life-changing magic of a long hike.

Fjellvettreglene (Norwegian Mountain Code)

The Norwegian Mountain Code contains the guidelines for having a safe trip in the Norwegian mountains. They're considered an important part of Norwegian cultural heritage and were introduced after a spate of fatal accidents in 1950.

1. Plan your trip and inform others about the route you have selected.

2. Adapt the planned routes according to ability and conditions.

3. Pay attention to the weather and the avalanche warnings.

4. Be prepared for bad weather and frost, even on short trips.

5. Bring the necessary equipment so you can help yourself and others.

6. Choose safe routes. Recognize avalanche terrain and unsafe ice.

7. Use a map and a compass. Always know where you are.

8. Don't be ashamed to turn around

9. Conserve your energy and seek shelter if necessary.

In case of emergency, notify the police at 112. You can also call 911 or 999, and the dispatch will connect you to the correct service. Within the cabins, there are signs giving the coordinates of the cabins and the emergency numbers.

Sarah Rowe has solo hiked more than 3,500 kilometers across 21 countries, with a focus on Norway and Austria. When she's not out in the mountains, she's drinking coffee, writing about hiking on her blog, Solo Female Wanderer, or planning the next adventure. She lives in the northeastern United States, two kilometers from the Appalachian Trail.

Questions or comments? You can reach her at
sarah@solofemalewanderer.com.